Wild Tal[es] from the WILD

For the weary urban dweller, the verdant Mangala valley near the Bandipur National Park in Karnataka, would seem like a haven of peace and tranquillity. Appearances could not be more deceptive, as Saad Bin Jung discovered after forsaking his life in the city for a stone cottage in the valley. If the surrounding jungles were teeming with wildlife of every variety, the life that the humans of the area led was no less wild. Here, he recounts the adventures that he had with some of them: the leopard who moved into 'bison cottage', the dining hall cobra, the magnificent Mangala tiger, Torn Ears, the most-photographed gaur of his time, and the elephants whom he loved with a passion, Colonel Hathi, Jayaprakash and even the Right-chipped Tusker with his bullying ways, amongst them.

Not to be outdone were the members of the Kuruba tribe and other humans – Mr B, the family expert, the elderly manager with a raging libido, the gorgeous foreign girls who almost saw him booted out of the family – who came to share his life at Bush Betta, the wildlife resort that he set up in 1991.

Hair-raising and hilarious, these are stories that anyone who has had a taste of the wilds, or wished that they could, will enjoy, as much for their drama and comedy as for the many fascinating insights into animal behaviour that they convey. No less compelling is the message between the lines: the grandeur and beauty of India's forests, and the need to preserve them at all costs.

***

Saad Bin Jung has spent more than twenty years travelling through the forests of India and Africa. When ill health compelled him to give up his first career of professional cricket, he turned to his other passion – wildlife. Today, in addition to the Bush Betta resort, he also runs angling and adventure camps in different jungles and Bush Betta trekking adventures. A scion of the royal families of Pataudi and Bhopal and the Paigah Wali ud Dowla of Hyderabad, he was a member of the Wildlife Advisory Board of Karnataka and is in the forefront of the eco-tourism movement that strives to use tourism as an integral tool for conservation.

OTHER LOTUS TITLES :

Boman Desai	*A Woman Madly in Love*
Frank Simoes	*Frank Unedited*
Frank Simoes	*Frank Simoes' Goa*
Harinder Baweja (ed.)	*Most Wanted: Profiles of Terror*
J.N. Dixit (ed.)	*External Affairs: Cross-Border Relations*
M.J. Akbar	*India: The Siege Within*
M.J. Akbar	*Kashmir: Behind the Vale*
M.J. Akbar	*Nehru: The Making of India*
M.J. Akbar	*Riot after Riot*
M.J. Akbar	*The Shade of Swords*
M.J. Akbar	*By Line*
Meghnad Desai	*Nehru's Hero Dilip Kumar: In the Life of India*
Nayantara Sahgal (ed.)	*Before Freedom: Nehru's Letters to His Sister*
Rohan Gunaratna	*Inside Al Qaeda*
Rifaat Hussain, J.N. Dixit Julie Sirrs, Ajai Shukla Anand Giridharadas Rahimullah Yusufzai John Jennings	*Afghanistan and 9/11*
Eric S. Margolis	*War at the Top of the World*
Maj. Gen. Ian Cardozo	*Param Vir: Our Heroes in Battle*
Mushirul Hasan	*India Partitioned. 2 Vols*
Mushirul Hasan	*John Company to the Republic*
Mushirul Hasan	*Knowledge Power and Politics*
Prafulla Roy, trans. John W.Hood	*In the Shadow of the Sun*
Rachel Dwyer	*Yash Chopra: Fifty Years of Indian Cinema*
Satish Jacob	*From Hotel Palestine Baghdad*
Sujata S. Sabnis	*A Twist in Destiny*
V.N. Rai	*Curfew in the City*
Veena Sharma	*Kailash Mansarovar: A Sacred Journey*

FORTHCOMING TITLES :

Khushwant Singh	*Death at My Doorstep*
Duff Hart-Davis	*Honorary Tiger: The Life of Billy Arjan Singh*

Wild Tales from the WILD

SAAD BIN JUNG

foreword
MANSUR ALI KHAN, NAWAB OF PATAUDI

LOTUS COLLECTION
ROLI BOOKS

Lotus Collection

First published in 2005
The Lotus Collection
An imprint of
Roli Books Pvt. Ltd.
M-75, G.K. II Market, New Delhi 110 048
Phones: ++91 (011) 2921 2271, 2921 2782
2921 0886, Fax: ++91 (011) 2921 7185
E-mail: roli@vsnl.com
Website: rolibooks.com
Also at
Varanasi, Agra, Jaipur and the Netherlands

Author picture on back cover: Sangeeta Jung
Cover : Sneha Pamneja
Layout : Narendra Shahi

ISBN: 81-7436-358-0
Rs. 295

Typeset in Fairfield LH Light by Roli Books Pvt. Ltd. and printed at Anudha Printers, Noida (UP)

To the three most wonderful, beautiful, loving and selfless people in the world, my parents and my wife, for having sacrificed their lives to me.

Contents

Acknowledgements ix
Foreword xiii
Introduction xv
Map and General Information on Bandipur National Park *xx*
Mangala 3
A Difficult Welcome 23
A Tigress Family for Neighbours 33
An Unpleasant Bully 41
The First Safari 53
Torn Ears and Other Animals 60
The Sloth Bear of Kardi Betta 80
Killer 87
The Bandipur Elephants 101
The Mangala Tiger 118
Snakes and Other Anecdotes 135
Shampoo and Chocolate 146
The Human Jungle 152
Mr B: An Expert in the Family 161
Narrations of a Tribal Smuggler 170
Epilogue 200

Acknowledgements

First and foremost, I have to say that no woman would be mad enough to have lived with me in the bush the way my wife, Sangeeta, has done. I took her away from the comforts of a well-to-do family in the city and threw her into the jungles of South India. That Sangeeta has survived both the bush and me and we have managed to raise two wonderful children, is solely due to her efforts. Bush Betta, our resort, and the time I have been able to spend in the jungles, could not have been accomplished without her incredible and selfless support that has made this book possible.

Zoha, our daughter has patiently typed and corrected more than two hundred pages, adding some of her own. Shaaz, our son and firstborn has an uncanny knack of simplifying everything. He has helped me understand the simplicity of life and I have tried my best to take his advice on keeping the book simple and to the point.

My parents need a special mention, for it is they who came up with the idea of a book. I would come home and narrate my latest experiences in the jungle, and my father would always say that I should write a diary, else I would forget.

My maternal uncle, Mansur Ali Khan, the Nawab of Pataudi would insist that I be his bearer, whenever he would go into the bush. Needless to say we have had some truly amazing moments together that further solidified my desire to live in the wilds.

I am also indebted to Nanjundiah our faithful friend and staff member. The amount he has taught me in the jungles surpasses belief. Together we have spent many nights out and have faced grave dangers. He has always stood by me.

Special thanks are due to M.K. Appayya, the retired Chief Wildlife Warden of Karnataka. He gave me the opportunity to go into the forests for the first time and would always make time to explain the problems that beset forest management to me.

I also thank K.S.N. Chikeroor, the IGP (CID) Forest, along with his friends, the heads of the Special Task Force. Even though they could do little to support the ban on visitors, they at all times ensured my safety above all through the frightening Veerappan era.

No acnowledgement would be complete without the mention of a truly loyal friend. I would like to state that if it had not been for Gurupadappa Nagmarapalli, Minister for Forests in Karnataka, I would not have been able to spend as much time as I was able to do in the forests of this state. It was because of him that I was given the opportunity to work on the Wildlife Board of Karnataka.

No book would be complete without mentioning our staff and officers of the forest department, especially at the Bandipur forest office and at our home in Mangala. Srinivas, our lifeline to the kitchen, has worked at every bush camp that we have had. Sharad, Kumar and Jaga have supported us through thick and thin.

Apart from Nanjundiah, the people who have given me a lot but taken very little in return are Narendar, my friend, partner and director in business, Gundu the Kuruba and Pradeep our Malayali tribal boy. Syed, who ably looked after the office whilst I was on the computer, and Subhan, who handled our angling camp not to forget Mallesh, our camp manager, who is the only person I know who has survived the kick of a furious wild elephant mother, released me from the chores of business that enabled me to write this book. I have spent hours in the forest with Nanju, Gundu, Pradeep and Subhan and they were the ones who taught me everything in my formative years in the bush.

I thank my brother Aamer Bin Jung for being such an able elder brother and my companion on many of the earlier adventures of the Jung brothers in the bush. I have not included them here, because you would never believe them. Like the time when he drove the jeep into the Bada Talab, the big lake in Bhopal, one night, in pursuit of two eyes that suddenly disappeared, but not before we were chest high in water! He thought it was a jackal that we were following and it turned out to be a crane!

It would take another book to mention the name of every person who has helped me and supported me in my quest to be in the wilds and in writing this book. It does not mean that if their names are not listed here, that I am not thankful to them. I am eternally grateful to one and all.

Finally this book would never have been possible had it not been for the timely support of M.J. Akbar, Editor-in-Chief, *Asian Age*, and Roli Books. Pramod Kapoor, Roli's publisher, agreed with MJ that maybe something could come out of the messy manuscript that I sent them and Renuka Chatterjee, my editor, worked overtime to ensure that the chaos got transformed into a book. I thank the three for believing in me and supporting me through every step of writing and editing this book.

Foreword

Saad Bin Jung is the second of four boys my sister brought into this world over a period of fifteen years. All four brothers were into sports, especially cricket, and jungle camp life in a big way, but only Saad and Aamir, his elder brother, got a glimpse of the variety and extent of wild life that existed even outside the sanctuaries and the game parks of this country. Today the pressure of population and destruction of their habitats has localized most of the wild animals in India within restrictive areas. I suppose some of this was inevitable, though a lack of concern and further surrender to the greed of the poacher/smuggler mafia will destroy forever some of the finest forests and wild life in the world.

In the years before 1972, it was possible to book a forest block in UP with one of those quaint 'dak' bungalows built by the British for ridiculously low prices. The package would include a cook, a cleaner, and a forest guard to show you around. This I did for a few days during the winter months, and took along sundry nephews and cousins for a bit of family bonding. One also took along a gun, but this was mainly for protection, for by the late '60s, the game had virtually disappeared from these public blocks. The incident with the tiger and myself that Saad writes about, which is not inaccurate, happened on one of these excursions.

Saad often came on these annual forays and even as a child, he was curious and interested in the relationship between man and animal when they shared the same space and lived in close proximity to one another. This interest was to turn into a passion. Meanwhile as he grew older, Saad also developed into a first class cricketer with his efforts culminating in an eyecatching hundred against the West Indies at Pune in 1978. He then fell seriously ill, which put him out of the reckoning for serious cricket. I have often been asked if he was good enough to play for his country. I am not sure but I do know of lesser players who have managed to represent India.

After his marriage in 1986, Saad somehow convinced his wife to move to Bangalore and set up a camp in the forest of Bandipur, a good five hours' drive away from the city. There was no road, no electricity, no telephone and no water, but there was an abundance of animals and several tribal hamlets. Although I never heard any complaints, the early years must have been rough with much work and little income, but in time Bush Betta, as the camp is named, has moved on to the tourist map. Saad is doing what he enjoys most, introducing his guests and family to elephants, leopards, deer, the odd tiger, and the village folk of the neighbourhood. He is often accompanied by his children and a long-resigned and loving wife. They are now a feature of the Bandipur-Madhumalai forest reserves, and very much a part of the development of tourism and wild life conservation of the State of Karnataka.

New Delhi
December 2004

Mansur Ali Khan,
Nawab of Pataudi

Introduction

And somehow you're sick of the highway, with its noise and its easy needs,
And you seek the risk of the by-way and reck not where it leads.

– R.W. Service

In 1970, when I was a young and exuberant student, all of ten years, I was asked to be the acting gun bearer of Mansur Ali Khan, the Nawab of Pataudi, my uncle and favourite shikari. As with other hunting stories, this one also is from a time when shooting was permitted under licence. It was the middle of winter in North India and we had driven to a small scrub jungle a good ten hours drive from Delhi. All I remember today is that we had gone shooting for wildfowl near the India-Nepal border and it had been freezing cold. That morning we were to shoot in a beat where the birds would be driven through the scrub and the hunters would have to take quick shots as they sailed past.

I never did enjoy shooting but I loved being with my childhood idol, and I was thrilled to do even the menial job of carrying his gun as he smoked a cigarette or was busy with some such important task.

The haka (beat) had started and we could hear the people beating the bush as they approached us with deliberate noise.

The hunters knew that it would be a while before the birds would be flushed out, as their initial run is on the ground and only when they feel really threatened do they take to the air.

At this point of time the Nawab had an urgent need to answer the call of nature. Not knowing what monsters would emerge from the deep woods he gave me his 12-bore and bade me to sit next to him as he took off his trousers and hung them on a branch nearby. He had just begun operations when we saw a huge tiger jump into the beat barely twenty yards from where we were sitting.

We had been assured that this jungle held no such fearsome beasts. The Nawab, topnotch sportsman that he was, was a very agile mover and realizing that the impossible had happened, took off for the jeep that was parked sixty yards from us at a gallop, leaving his trousers behind. He dived inside the jeep as soon as he reached it.

Meanwhile having witnessed the fast receding, naked royal backside of the cricket captain of India, I completely forgot the grave threat of a disturbed tiger that stared me in the face, and collapsed in a state of hysteria. My cousins found me thus, rolling on the ground with laughter. I like to think that the tiger shared my mirth, which is why he didn't attack me! Such was my introduction to the wilds of India. I daresay even after all these years in the jungles, I have never come upon a funnier incident. Such episodes and other exciting – and some terrifying – events in the bush during my formative years, created a love and zest for the wilderness that is alive and thriving till today.

I grew up in the jungles around Bhopal. My grandmother, Her Highness Mehr Taj Begum Sajida Sultan, being the ruler of the state did help for we had numerous shikar gahs spread around the jungles of Bhopal state. Those holidays that we did not spend in Bhopal, we spent in Pataudi, a village near Gurgaon, with my aforementioned uncle, Mansur Ali Khan, and his family. This included his wife, Begum Ayesha Sultan Sharmila Tagore, and his son, Saif Ali Khan, now a well-known actor.

Near Bhopal were the family hunting lodges. Chiklod, Khajuri, Delawari are some names that I remember from the past. Chiklod was of course the most enjoyable as it was built in a valley surrounded by hills and overlooking a beautiful lake.

The ruler's shikar gah or hunting lodge is not an ordinary place. It is laid out to ensure that when the ruler does spend time here, he or she can manage the state and still have the best of luxuries. Thus staff quarters, guest rooms, some with the staircase made solely from sambar antlers, swimming pool, a tennis court and even a zoo were a few of the facilities that existed. Thus I grew up with jungles in my blood.

Whenever my elder brother Aamer and I were not in the bush we were playing cricket. Whether it was in our house, road, palace, or even the drawing room, we played cricket and our parents allowed us to break everything that was there to be broken. I still remember Test players from the West Indies, England and India playing in the veranda of our Hyderabad house. People and players would come home for dinner and out would come the tennis ball and cricket bat. Would that ever happen with today's players?

From the very beginning, wildlife and cricket shared an equal footing in my life. Initially, I thought it was through cricket that I could build my fortunes. I had been batting for school, playing C-Division league cricket when, one day, I saw a car drive in and stay through my innings. Only later was I told that it was M.L. Jaisimha, the retired legendary captain of Hyderabad who had come especially to see me.

Things then took a fast turn for me careerwise. Before long, I was selected to play the All India invitation Moin-ud-Dowla tourney and having impressed the selectors, went on to play the under-19 and under-22 for my state of Hyderabad and the South Zone. Opening with the likes of K. Srikkant made cricket a great game to play. Finally, I was chosen to play for India under-22 versus the West Indies. Subsequently, I played against Australia and Pakistan and have played the first class circuit in India. I also played in England.

Cricket at this point looked like a truly good prospect as a career. I was signing autographs and living the life of a celebrity, stopping traffic and turning heads as I went by, being invited to functions and, in the short time that I played, even managing a fan following.

Then I fell ill. I was in and out of hospitals for two years. My illness put paid to any hopes that I may have had of reaching the first few steps of the incredible achievements of my uncle on the cricket field, and even though I still have newspaper clippings about those days, my cricketing days were over. I turned to my other passion, the jungle.

There used to be a small hamlet, which of late has become a village, surrounded by the thick jungles of Bandipur, called Mangala. In this live the people of the Kuruba tribe who share the valley with the animals of the Bandipur National Park. It took six years for my dream of being involved with wildlife to come true, and that was when I arrived in Mangala. I have spent over forty years visiting different jungles but have stayed in the Bandipur area the longest. I have made it a point to travel the African bush extensively and have managed to see as much as I would have liked. Today I can say with sincerity that I have worked the African bug out of my system but there was a time when I thought of settling in Africa.

I have grown to know both the animals and tribals of the area and have spent enough time in their company to know that their lives are involved in an endless struggle for survival, and there is a severe conflict evolving. I have also spent enough time with both sides to fall head over heels in love with each and every one of them, be it an animal or a human. Sadly I have come to realize that it is a lose-lose situation for both sides. I try and do what I can to ensure that the loss is minimal and spread over the longest duration. This passage of time might help the forest administration to come up with solutions that will enable both the tribal and the animals to live in harmony as they once did many years ago.

Sangeeta, my wife and I had a choice between Madhumalai, Bandipur and the Nilgiris for us to move and settle. We chose Bandipur because it was unspoilt by urban man. That it was plundered and devastated by rural man and the tribal was something that we learnt only much later.

Which brings me to the partner in my wild life. It was in the Secunderabad Club, back home in Hyderabad, that I met the woman of my dreams. I wooed her with a bouquet of bougainvillea flowers plucked from the fence of the club. She accepted my offer of a date and was soon funding the first of the many dinners that we have had together since. My contribution to our entire courtship being three 180 ml bottles of red wine. Within a week of our first date, she asked me to marry her, or so I would like to believe. Sangeeta was not only gorgeous but also a spirited woman willing to risk the rest of her life with a mad hatter like me.

The stories in this book are based on my experiences in the bush. Some are semi-fictionalized stories in the lives of the animals and people that I have known whilst the rest are true accounts of some of my personal experiences. People similar to the ones I have described exist in the valley and all the tracks and waterholes that have been named are still there. You can still walk these paths and meet the animals and the people that have made my life so complete.

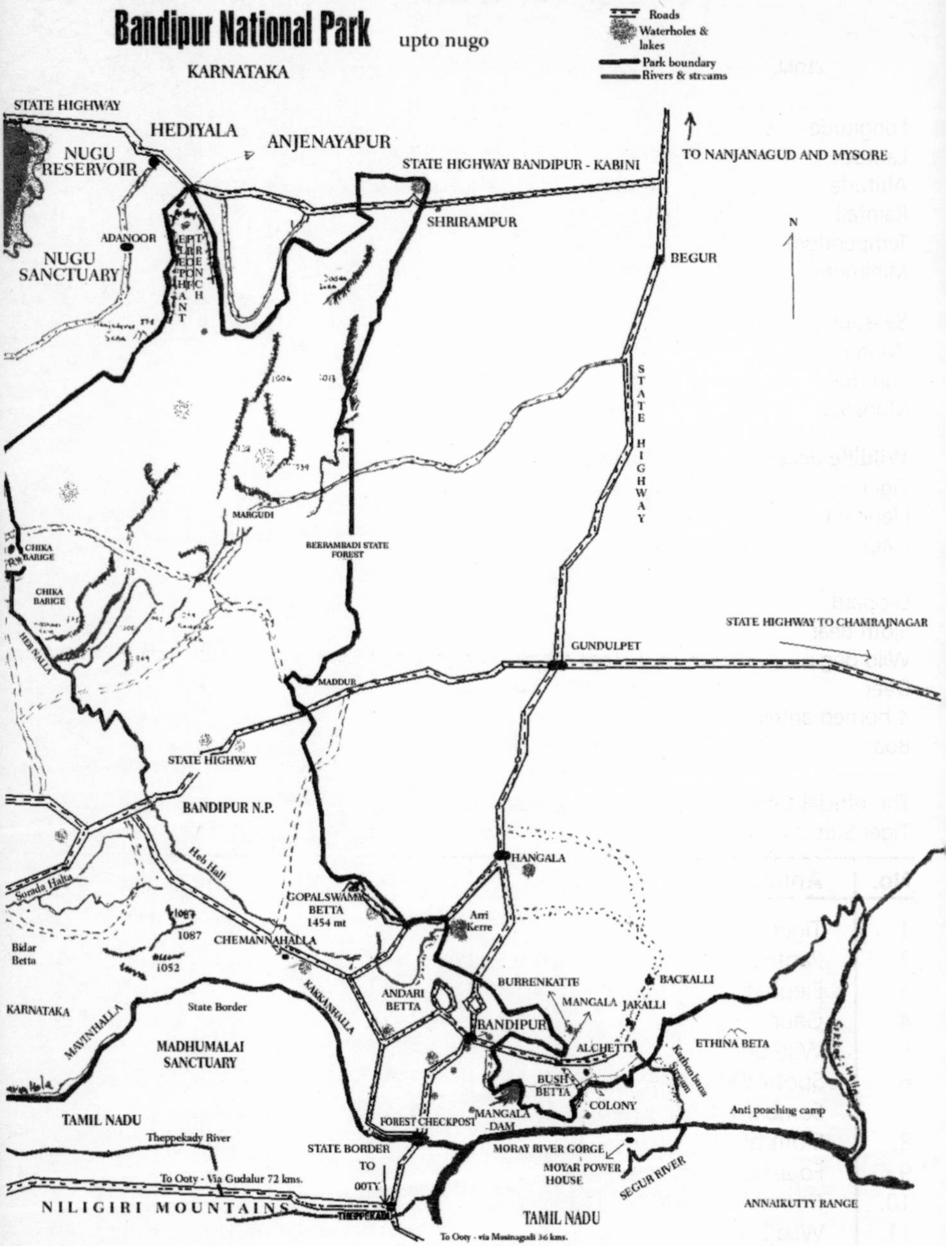

Bandipur National Park

upto nugo

KARNATAKA

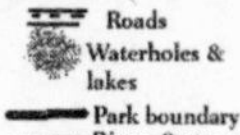

STATE HIGHWAY

HEDIYALA

NUGU RESERVOIR

ANJENAYAPUR

STATE HIGHWAY BANDIPUR - KABINI

TO NANJANAGUD AND MYSORE

SHRIRAMPUR

ADANOOR

NUGU SANCTUARY

N

BEGUR

STATE HIGHWAY

MARGUDI

BEERAMBADI STATE FOREST

CHIKA BARIGE

CHIKA BARIGE

HEB HALLA

STATE HIGHWAY TO CHAMRAJNAGAR

GUNDULPET

MADDUR

STATE HIGHWAY

BANDIPUR N.P.

Heb Hall

Sorada Halla

HANGALA

GOPALSWAMI BETTA 1454 mt

Arri Kerre

1087

CHEMANNAHALLA

Bidar Betta

1052

BURRENKATTE

BACKALLI

ANDARI BETTA

MANGALA

JAKALLI

KARNATAKA

State Border

MAVINHALLA

KAKKANHALLA

BANDIPUR

ETHINA BETA

MADHUMALAI SANCTUARY

ALCHETTY

BUSH BETTA

COLONY

Anti poaching camp

TAMIL NADU

FOREST CHECKPOST

MANGALA DAM

Theppekady River

STATE BORDER

MORAY RIVER GORGE

TO OOTY

MOYAR POWER HOUSE

SEGUR RIVER

To Ooty - Via Gudalur 72 kms.

NILIGIRI MOUNTAINS

THEPPEKADU

TAMIL NADU

ANNAIKUTTY RANGE

To Ooty - via Masinagudi 36 kms.

General Information on Bandipur National Park

Area *: Core - 523 sq. km. | Buffer - 357 sq. km. | Total - 880 sq. km.*

Longitude	:	75° 12′ 17″ E to 76° 51′ 32″ E
Latitude	:	11° 35′ 34″ N to 11° 57′ 02″ N
Altitude	:	780 m – 1454.5 m above msl.
Rainfall	:	625 mm. to 1250 mm.
Temperature	:	Maximum: 29° C
Minimum	:	10° C

Seasons

Winter	:	November to mid-February
Summer	:	February to mid-May
Monsoon	:	End May to September

Wildlife Seasons for Best Sightings

Tiger	:	Dry months of summer
Elephant	:	From May to mid-February
Gaur	:	From May to mid-February. (Might move in Earlier depending on the April showers)
Leopard	:	Through the year
Sloth bear	:	Monsoons
Wild dogs	:	Through the year
Deer	:	Through the year
4 horned antelope	:	Through the year
Boar	:	Through the year

The official Census figures are enclosed herein. Census as taken from the 2001 Project Tiger Status available with the Ministry of Environment and Forests is given below:

No.	Animal	1991	1993	1995	1997
1.	Tiger	58	66	74	75
2.	Panther	51	81	86	88
3.	Elephant	1107	2214	2214	3471
4.	Gaur	1097	1373	1373	2427
5.	Wild dog	148	181	181	–
6.	Spotted deer	3333	5858	5858	8204
7.	Sambar	706	1196	1196	2386
8.	Sloth bear	51	66	66	–
9.	Four-horned antelope	14	–	–	–
10.	Common langur	1468	1751	1751	–
11.	Wild boar	148	181	181	–
12.	Barking deer	72	131	131	–
13.	Mouse deer	–	–	–	–
14.	Porcupine	–	–	–	–
15.	Chital	–	–	–	8204

. . . but in her heart of hearts
she is and remains wild and
free and unaffected by the
invading influences.

– J.C. Smuts

Mangala

I passed through a paper village under glass
Where the explorers first found silence and taught it to speak.

– Richard Sheldon

Before we get to Mangala, my home in the beautiful wilds of Bandipur in the state of Karnataka, there is a story I would like to tell about an incident that occurred in the Laikipia plateau of Kenya.

I had gone to Kenya in 1996 to meet a few consultant friends who were trying to sell Indian wildlife holiday packages to the Kenyans. There were three of them. If you were ever to encounter wildlife in the city, it would have to be them. Prem Marcus, whom I can only describe as a better-looking version of Aravinda de Silva, the Sri Lankan batsman, was the leader. Excellent at his job, extremely disciplined and aggressive. Shayne Ross was short compared to his boss, very round and very fat. He was the party animal who knew every nightclub in Nairobi. Then there was Mr Cool – the ever dependable and gentle Dominic.Women did not overly excite him, like they did the others, and he would be content to sit in a corner with a drink and a smoke. The first and the last time I ever smoked in my life, was in the heart of the Masai Mara – playing chess with Dominic. That it was a reefer I found only after I saw two suns setting in the ever-beautiful African horizon.

The three had never been into the African wilds and on my arrival, they implored me to take them to a few sanctuaries. We chose to visit the Sweet Water camp that lies at an altitude of around 6,000 feet above sea level on the high Laikipia plateau, literally on the equator and overlooking the snowcapped Mount Kenya, the abode of the Masai god Engai. A view of elephants and giraffe silhouetted against the snow peaks of Mount Kilimanjaro or Mount Kenya is one of the most hauntingly beautiful sights that a person can ever experience.

We arrived at the camp in our borrowed 'combi' Volkswagen van in the early afternoon and decided to take off immediately for a drive into the huge fenced-in conservation area. Not knowing the terrain and the routes we asked the camp to loan us a guide and a driver. We were given a strapping middle-aged Samburu guide and a lean Masai youngster called Peter as the driver.

We must have driven a few kilometres when I saw the bull elephant grazing in the open grassland.

I asked Peter to drive around him in order to keep the cloud-covered Mount Kenya in the background, and then switch off the engine as I took my fill of photos of the magnificent creature.

That day either the gods had clashed or the elephant was in a bad mood, for he chose not to accommodate the tourists from across the seas. No sooner had the van come to a standstill than he began to show his agitation. Swaying from side to side, he started on a ritual of kicking the small tufts of grass with increasing fervour. It was when his body started to shake to and fro and shudder with anger that I asked Peter to start the van and be ready for a quick getaway. I knew from experience in the Indian bush that the animal was going to charge. Sure enough, I had barely finished speaking when he let out a shrill threatening trumpet and with ears flying high and trunk tucked in tight, came charging straight at the van.

I was busy taking pictures when I realized that the animal was filling up my lens and that even by zooming out to the full, I could not get the entire elephant in the frame. The ground below us was trembling, the vibrations reaching my hands resting on the van's roof. The elephant finished his first charge barely six yards from us and in his first rush itself I felt his spittle spatter my face and the lens.

As he stood over us, a glowering giant with ears outstretched, a mean gurgle escaping his trunk, I heard the click of the left door opening and the sound of running feet. That is when I realized why the van had not started. Peter, our Masai driver, had bolted – and so had our Samburu guide! Having been deserted by tribals in India in similar situations, I wasn't really surprised.

When I heard the back door sliding I realized that my companions also had the same idea and were preparing to throw themselves headlong into flight, away from this terrible ordeal to which I was subjecting them. Knowing that they would surely be killed if the elephant were to see them, I grabbed at Prem's trousers and yanked him back, screaming at them not to be foolish and to stay in the vehicle. I forced both Prem and Dominic onto the back seat and told Shayne Ross to start the van.

Meanwhile the elephant was on his fourth charge and after every attack, it appeared to me that he was getting closer. By now I was sweating and my insides were churning. But I knew I had to arrest the rising panic and do something fast, for past experience had taught me that it was critical to stop the initial charges as it is this first onrush that carries the maximum adrenaline that may lead to contact. The subsequent ones are normally of less intensity. Even armed with this knowledge I was terrified. Animals in the wild quite often do not follow set patterns, and the elephant was acting anything but normal. At that moment it had seemed to me that it was now only a matter of time before the big bull smashed the van.

That was when Shayne Ross dropped the bomb and declared in a shaky voice that he could not find the key. He whispered that maybe Peter had taken it with him as he fled. Ross stands up well to pressure and that day I saw him master his panic. Under the menacing charges of the large bull elephant he somehow managed to spot the key lying a few feet from the van on the ground. Staying hidden behind the vehicle he crept out to fetch it and dived back into the combi.

But in the bush, when things decide to go wrong, they do so wholesale. The poor Volkswagen had already taken a beating at Shayne's hands for just before we came upon the elephant, he had taken the wheel for a while. He had braked hard to avoid a rhino, essayed a 360-degree turn and had been swept clean of the wet road into the jungle. An astonished and visibly upset rhino had circled and danced around the van for a few minutes, trying to decide whether he should exterminate its occupants or ignore them. Luckily, with head held high, he had chosen to trot away into the thorny acacia bush.

Now, with the elephant destroying the African soil in front of us, the engine of the old beauty chose not to start. It was as if the vehicle had a mind of its own and was throwing a sulk of mammoth proportions. It was only after a lot of coaxing, sweet talking, cursing and finally kicking, that it fired and we fled from the scene in great haste.

This incident proves two things: that wildlife anywhere in the world can be dangerous and also that the tourist guides at the Sweet Water camp in Laikipia were not trained in handling animals that behaved in a hostile and eccentric manner – something I encountered elsewhere in Africa as well. To me it appeared that here the wilderness had been typecast to fit a particular image and when it deviated from this conception, then the average African (here I do admit that maybe I have met the wrong Africans so far) was unable to handle this change in the animal's attitude.

The fact remains that had we had a similar experience in the Indian jungle, I do not think we would have got away alive. I do not mean to say that the wilds of India are more dangerous than Africa for that would be incorrect, but I feel with my experience in both jungles, I can hazard a guess that the wild animals of India are quite possibly fiercer than their counterparts in Africa, especially when it comes to their relationship with the human race. The Indian elephant charges with more regularity and ferociousness. During an attack, where the African elephant will more often than not, veer off at the last moment, the chances are greater that the Indian elephant will actually make contact. The elephant at Sweet Water had broken the safety barrier that pachyderms in India prefer to keep between them and the humans, even when they attack – which from my experience, is around eight to ten yards. Yet the African elephant had chosen not to make contact with the combi.

The reason for this may be the smaller tracts of forests available in India for the elephants to roam in compared with the large expanses found in Africa. A national park of 1,500 square kilometres would be considered really large in India whereas in Africa it would be the size of a private concession. National parks in Africa can be well above 15,000 square kilometres in area. Thus the man-animal conflict takes on a more serious form in India.

The Indian jungle can be a devastatingly beautiful friend and at the same time a deceptively deadly adversary. 'You shall live only as long as you respect your enemy,' is an old jungle saying. In Mangala, I have learnt to love and respect not only the persons who live in the valley but also the animals that have chosen to make this haven a part of their life.

***

Many moons ago, in the early '80s, Mangala was a small hamlet mainly inhabited by jungle people of the Kuruba tribe, with the exception of a few powerful Lingayat and Gowda families who controlled the valley. Mangala is a Kannada word that when translated into English means good, upright, virtuous and moral. Life in the village at first appeared to signify just these virtues but it was not till I had spent time in Mangala that I realized that life here was anything but virtuous.

By jeep Mangala was five kilometres from the office of the Deputy Director, Project Tiger - Bandipur. There were no cars in the valley and the tribal would measure distance in time. It took barely an hour and fifteen minutes of brisk walking through some incredibly pretty and wild country, full of big game, before one arrived in the village.

The Mangala valley lies at the base of the Nilgiris otherwise known as the Blue Mountains of South India. It is surrounded by low-lying undulating hills with the distant mountains visible to the south of the village.

It is at the centre of a large tract of forest that extends from Coorg in the west to the Cauvery Wildlife Division in the north-east. Even though the river Moyar flows only a few kilometres to the south of the village, access to the water is impossible, as the river has cut a huge trench, around a thousand feet deep, in the plateau. This trench, called the Moyar ditch, is a hub of illegal activity. It forms the natural boundary between the states of Karnataka and Tamil Nadu. On the south is a hydropower-generating unit, which feeds the Nilgiris, and the northern side is still comparatively wild.

Apart from the Moyar, there are no other major rivers in the Mangala valley. There is a small stream, which is basically a run off from the Mangala dam and then there is the perennial stream called Kathenburra that bisects the valley. But this is well after the village of Mangala. Most people here live a life of leisure for half the year and do overtime for the rest, as they rely solely on rain for their cultivation.

Mangala has hilly forested tracts on all sides and big game can be found on every hill. The villagers, for whom life is a constant struggle against the hardships of everyday living, would raid these jungles for forest produce. Be it smuggling or poaching, right or wrong, the unwritten rule was that at least one member of the family be dedicated to this work, as the household needed to survive the six months of drought.

The forest suffered under the impact of their illegal activities and the bush thinned over a period of time. But nature has its own way of getting even and when it hits back, it devastates. So it was with Mangala. Till date professional field raiders, consisting of large herds of around twenty-six elephants, pillage the sparse crop cultivated by the tribals and others of the valley. This is apart from the lone elephant bulls, sambar, chital, bear, leopard, wild boar and sometimes even the tiger, that plunder their fields and livestock.

It has always been tough living for the people of the Kuruba tribe and it is getting tougher still with time. But one man's loss is another's gain. The valley is heaven for a visitor from the city, whose every sense has been polluted by urban smog and who is unable to see the conflict in the short time that he spends in these areas.

Lying as it does at the foothills of the Nilgiris, the average height of Bandipur is around 3,200 feet above sea level. At Bandipur (where the government tourism complex is situated), opposite the police station, there used to be a mud track which has since been tarred. It was quite unobtrusive and insignificant to a city dweller and it looked like any of the game drive tracks that abound in the tourism zone of the park. I was the first entrepreneur to take this path and the valley has been my home ever since.

It was by pure luck that I discovered the valley, in the winter of 1985. Kishore Mallya, a good friend who also happened to be my lawyer, and I had decided to head for the bush to drown our sorrows. I was then an unsuccessful consultant involved in running a distribution network which had been fraught with all kinds of illegal dealings that can only be possible in the rather conducive environment of the Third World. We had just lost a sales tax appeal for my principals and both lawyer and client were smarting under the humiliation, for that is how the industry saw it, of having to pay a large sum of money to the government. The fresh air and unpolluted environment of the jungles of South India would, we hoped, refresh our souls and rejuvenate our spirits.

On a cool December morning, we left Bangalore at noon. No sooner had we crossed Mysore, than we came across huge heaps of grass lying on the road. We managed to avoid most, only to be met by angry looks and oaths from the villagers we passed along the way. Not till we saw a bus drive at breakneck speed over these mounds did we realize what we were supposed to do. The villagers were separating the grain from the ragi stalks. Ragi is the staple diet of the Kannadigas and is grown in profusion in the south. It is extremely healthy to eat, fat free and full of roughage.

Initially, it was with some hesitation that Kishore drove his brand new Premier Padmini Fiat over these mounds. But after a few had been successfully dealt with, without any apparent damage to the car, we were soon speeding with great aplomb over the stalks, much to the delight of the waving villagers. We waved back, happy that we were doing our good deed for the day. Only later would we realize our folly.

We had reserved a room at the tourist complex at Bandipur and were looking forward to the next three days with a sense of adventure. We must have been the only guests staying in the complex and to us it seemed that we had achieved what most urban humanity had failed to even imagine. An understanding and respect for solitude and peace.

We entered the forest and drove past a sign with the picture of a tiger welcoming the traveller with a caption that read, 'Do not look at me in that tone of voice.' Having registered at the reception we walked to our room which turned out to be the last of the wooden cottages, built in line to offer maximum game sighting from the bars of the windows. It was very regimental and very government.

It was late evening by then, and we relaxed on our veranda awed by the sounds of the jungle. We heard the wild fowl bidding good night and the sound of a thousand hooves as huge herds of chital moved into camp. We listened in wonder to the elephants roaring, for roar they do, as night settled onto the camp.

We knew we were embarking on something special. Silently we revelled in the excitement of the exploration, content in the fact that we had it all to ourselves.

The thought of sharing this moment with any other person was sacrilege. My feelings even for the forest officers, who risked their lives trying to conserve this wilderness, were tinged with jealousy. Little did I know that one day not too far away, I would be taking this very solitude to all the people who wanted a taste of this wonderful wilderness, and make a life for myself by allowing them to share the jungles with me.

That night, sitting on the cane chair outside the cottage, knowing full well that I would never be able to own the forests, I seriously made believe that I did. It was only when I truly belonged to the area that I lost the need to possess. But this took years of pain and turmoil.

The morning drive did not have great game viewing but being in the forests was enough. Just feeling the cool wet wind ruffling my hair was bliss. Brown and shaggy sambar, graceful spotted deer and their symbiotic relationship with the langur were glimpses of a truly healthy eco-biosphere. As we drove down the dusty roads of Bandipur, we could feel our tensions drain away.

Unlike the big five in Africa, India has the big six. These in my view are the tiger, leopard, elephant, rhino, Indian gaur and the wild buffalo. I am tempted to add both wild dogs and sloth bear to the list, but they are not quite as majestic. Bandipur offers great sighting of four of the big six but we were unlucky not to see any on our first foray into the jungle.

We returned to camp with an unquenched thirst, a thirst that would stay with me for life. That morning, after a quick breakfast, we set off in the car to explore further.

It was with many a hard-fought battle in court that Kishore had paid for the Premier Padmini. Its sturdy and shining chassis filled us with confidence. We asked the tribal waiting on us for a route that we could investigate without getting into trouble. For driving on jungle tracks without department permission was and still is, illegal. Why just show us the way, the tribal, who said that he had plenty of time to spare, decided to come with us as he had work in another village not far from camp. Packing our instant camera (that was all we possessed then), we set off on our exploration.

Opposite the Bandipur police outpost, we turned left onto a dirt track. The tribal explained that this road was under the control of the revenue department as it led to a few villages. There was even a daily bus service on this route and it was at an unlicensed local liquor dealer's house in one of these hamlets that he had to be dropped off. He would take the milk lorry and stagger back to Bandipur by evening.

The track heads east and dips into a culvert as you leave Bandipur. The culvert is over a dry nallah filled with thick bamboo on either side. Under the bridge are two large cement pipes that allow the water through. Little did I know that one day, these pipes would save my life! After the narrow furrow, the road climbs for about 300 yards and then evens out after it bends slightly to the south. Eucalyptus has been planted in this part of the forest and can be seen growing in profusion on both sides of the track. Just a little further and at right angles to the road, heading right, was a game track which seemed to run straight into the jungle for a kilometre and then turn and dip to the right as it disappeared into thick foliage. This we were told led to a dam that had water throughout the year. I saved this bit of information as being important. Barely a hundred yards to the left from this turn off is another track that leads into the valley, heading due north. The tribal explained that it ran down to a fire divide and then formed the dividing line, which separates the forest from revenue and private lands. He said both these tracks were full of game.

It was at the branch off to the dam that I asked Kishore to turn the car and head for the big water. At this the tribal stiffened and warned us not to do so, as it was dangerous. I asked him to forget about the danger, for that we could tackle in the new car but did enquire if the forest officials had closed this route. A hesitant 'no' from the tribal was enough to see us hurtling down the game track towards the dam.

Call it the silliness of youth or the folly of inexperience, but hurtle we did straight into danger.

We had hardly gone a kilometre when the track turned right and headed down into a thick bamboo clump. We were out to see the big six, and it was the biggest of them that we saw. Bang in the middle of the road, was a huge, grey mass of flesh, and it was thundering down upon us. The sounds that it was making were unlike anything we had ever heard before. All I remember thinking was that this was a very non-elephant like sound and a very unfriendly situation that we had got ourselves into.

My lawyer friend and I were stunned into inactivity. We were terrified and sat dumbfounded as the elephant charged the car head on. He was making so much noise that we barely heard the click of the back door opening. It was the sound of running tribal feet that shook us into action. Not knowing what to say but knowing that we had to get out of the danger zone I screamed at Kishore to reverse. There was gratification in the grating sound of the gear being forced into reverse. We were jerked forward as the car shot backwards.

On that ominous December morning, luck was not favouring the brave. The car stopped with a shudder. I thought at first that we had stalled. It is not uncommon, under grave duress, to release the clutch much quicker than the engine is designed for, only to find oneself stationary in front of fast approaching death.

I yelled at my friend to restart and move, for by now the ugly, mean mass of flesh was not more than twenty yards from us. Kishore, who used to be an opening batsman like me, who had fought many nerve-wracking battles in court, restarted the car and released the clutch only to find that the wheels had jammed and the car refused to budge.

Cold sweat poured out of every pore, and even on that cool morning my shirt was drenched. I knew then that the axle had got jammed with the ragi stalks and we were in the middle of a life-threatening crisis. Kishore, realizing that the car was not going to move and that we were going to get bludgeoned by two tons of angry elephant decided, like the tribal, to make a run for it.

Something warned me that running was the wrong thing to do. And just as he was about to jump out of the door, I grabbed his belt and yanked him back into the car. His shoulder struck the steering and jammed on the horn. The sudden blast from the shrill new horn surprised the charging pachyderm. Seeing his hesitation, I knew in a flash what our next course of action should be.

I ordered Kishore not to leave the car but to blast the horn, stick his neck out of the window and scream at the top of his voice. Kishore yelled back saying I had broken his shoulder and was flexing his arm to biff me in the face. I had no idea that I was under threat from the lawyer and even if I had known I couldn't have cared much about a minor alteration to my face. Approaching us was an animal that is known to push people on the ground and then, putting his foot on their chests, pull out their limbs and fling them high into the trees. Just as I got my head out of the window, the elephant screamed. This brought Kishore back to his senses and forgetting me for the moment, he followed suit. It must have been bravery born out of desperation that forced both our heads out of the car that day.

We were stunned by the apparition that was bearing down on us. It is only from up close that one can appreciate the incredible power and size of these animals and when the animal is upset and within a few yards of you, then believe me when I tell you that it is by far the most frightening sight that you will ever see in your life. We screamed. We screamed in sheer terror. We screamed in sheer helplessness. We screamed and we blasted the horn and opened the car door to make it look bigger and waved our hands. The elephant was ten yards from the bonnet when he braked. There was hardly any dust but I recollect the car being peppered by flying gravel as the pachyderm came to a standstill. I remember his saliva flying onto the windscreen and I remember Kishore Mallya yelling. Yes, he yelled like never before, he yelled heartily, for a short but gutsy man was he.

Slowly our screams changed in tenor and soon we were yelling in triumph for the elephant, not knowing what kind of madness awaited him if he were to make contact with the car, broke and ran.

It was a tribal rolling on the ground with laughter, that we found after the elephant had departed. The tribal told us that he had never witnessed anything like that morning and not being an experienced guide had chosen to run. I realized later that the tribal runs instinctively, whenever charged by a wild animal. Only extensive training and the need to protect the tourists have changed this inbred behaviour. He said that he would never forget what he saw from the vantage of a tall tree.

What he had seen was an elephant repeatedly attacking a puny car, which had its doors opening and closing and two heads sticking out of the windows, screaming utter gibberish.

Initially he had been worried for the occupants of the vehicle and for himself, for had anything happened, he would surely have been in trouble with the forest ranger. But once it became clear that the elephant was not going to press home the attack and make contact, the entire episode took on the hue of a vaudeville act.

I still remember the gooseflesh on my skin, the perspiration drenching me through and through, and my heart hammering my ribcage. But then I also remember a sense of accomplishment for we had stopped the huge animal from killing us.

It was yet another cheap lesson learnt very early in my life in the bush. I call it cheap because most incidents in the bush are prone to have a sad ending. Normally the human, being the weakest of the animals in the forests, carrying no weapons for self-protection, would land up getting himself killed or if he were lucky, maimed or injured if a wild animal did attack him.

The lesson we learnt was simple – when in a severe crisis with a wild animal in the bush and when all exit routes have been sealed and fleeing is no longer an option, then stand your ground and call the animal's bluff. And then – pray. Chances are you will spook the attacker and get away without harm, injury or even death. Today I know, from many years of experience in the bush that had we moved back and shown submission, the elephant would most certainly have made contact with the car. And that is the way of the jungle. Things happen when you least expect them to and then it all depends on the person who is being subjected to the happening. If he does not panic and thinks coolly through the options available, then he could with luck, always with luck, walk away from a hair-raising experience.

It was after the elephant had sauntered away that we got under the car and saw the reason for the jamming of the wheels. My suspicion had been correct. The long stalks of ragi were entangled in the axis and had prevented the shaft from turning. It took considerable effort to slice away the stems with my Swiss knife. Eventually we got the car going and turned back toward the main road.

As we passed the fire line on the way to the hamlet, we realized that the foliage had changed. The jungles after the fire divide were bushy and without the normal tree cover.

We had just crossed the fire divide when we saw an old man ambling in the direction of the village which was still about two kilometres ahead. Our tribal guide whispered to us to give him a lift, for he was the tribal head of the valley. Mockingly I asked our guide why he was whispering, as there was no way the old man could hear us from where we were.

The tribal looked contemptuously at me and said that the old man knew and heard everything, for he travelled with the spirits of their ancestors. I chose not to reply and masked my amusement at the simplicity of these jungle people. I never imagined then that this same old man would become my greatest ally in the valley and would honour me by taking me with him to the realms of a life that I never knew existed. He was, I was to discover later, one of the very few, really extraordinary men that I would have the privilege of calling a good friend. For consequent to my settling down in the valley, I spent a long time with him in the bush, learning and absorbing the laws of the jungle. I learnt that the greatest threat to our forests is man himself. For when man decides to play god with things that are living, he more often than not makes a complete mess.

But on that day, having already experienced the pitfalls of giving the tribal a lift in Africa, I was hesitant to stop. Once, en route to Masai Mara, we had given two tribal women a lift from Narok to Paradise lodge. The next three days were spent cleaning the Volkswagen combi, for the raw earthy aroma that the two ladies left behind would not have been appreciated by the owner of the vehicle who had loaned it to us for the trip.

But Kishore, not having been party to the incident, drew up and let the old man into the car before I had time to warn him. The frail tribal was on his way to the same liquor shop in the village as our guide. He was a very small man with multiple lines of wisdom on his old and wrinkled face.

As we passed the forest boundary and drove on towards the village, the chief explained that these were private lands that the forest department had given to the tribals as part of their rehabilitation. He went on to enlighten us about the severe conflict that the people of this area had with both the forest department and the wildlife surrounding them. Most of the big trees had been cut and sold to make way for an abundance of thick bush. Since this bush is very rich in nutrition, large bovine herds would position themselves in its midst, ready to attack the cultivated fields of the valley at night. Thus by cutting the trees the people of the valley had actually attracted the large herds of herbivore to the fringes of the valley. With the herbivore came the carnivore. Thus the entire valley found itself surrounded by a threat that came in all kinds and sizes.

On the right about 500 yards from the dividing line is a big waterhole. I got down and walked on the periphery to look for spoor. What I saw amazed me. There were fresh tiger and leopard pugmarks, elephant spoor and heaps of elephant dung and all shapes and sizes of wild bovine hooves imprinted in the wet mud.

Leaving the waterhole behind, we travelled another kilometre on the track till we came to the edge of the bush – and entered heaven. It was a valley with a yellow carpet, surrounded by varying hues of green hills on all sides. Far to the south-east, through a small gap in the hills, I could see the Blue Mountains.

The entry to this valley was past another shallow pool to the right, which again was overflowing with the dung and scat of different species of wildlife. The more I drove into the glen the more I fell in love with it.

A kilometre from the waterhole was the small hamlet of Mangala. Today it is no longer a hamlet but a fully equipped village with its own granary, school, post office, telephone exchange and grocery shop.

The moment I saw the valley I told my friend the lawyer that this was where I wanted to spend the rest of my life. That very first day when I entered the valley, I decided that I would shut down my life in the city and invest whatever I had in a small piece of land and a house in the bush.

I had visions of a small wildlife lodge that would help me live with these beautiful people of the jungle and at the same time feed my family and maybe pay for their education. By small I meant really minuscule for I would barely be able to afford the land, let alone the lodge. All these thoughts flooded my mind as we drove through the valley. I knew I had walked into my dream valley, my flight of fancy, and that my pipe dream could just possibly become a reality.

The lawyer in Kishore warned me about the strict laws for buying agricultural land in Karnataka. Luckily, I had agricultural land in Andhra Pradesh and my papers were in order, which proclaimed me to be an agriculturist. I also knew that I had hardly any income to speak of from my job as a consultant with the distribution business, and so the law limitations would not apply to me. Sipping tea in the village, I explained my game plan to the lawyer and pleaded for his help in making it happen.

After having retired from first class cricket at the ripe age of twenty-one, and after my prolonged illness, this had been the first time that I had felt the familiar stirring of butterflies in the stomach. The tingling of nerves as you plunge into an unknown adventure. Every sportsman who has played the game at any competitive level knows what I am speaking of. Nothing quite compares with the thrill of the unknown as you partake in a sport that defines your passion. That is what I was experiencing as I sat and drank black tea in a small metal cup on the dusty road of Mangala.

Since then I have achieved my dream, I have my land and my wildlife resort, Bush Betta. I have my house, my tribals and my forests but I have lost my friend the lawyer. He left me without warning. Knowing that he has given me my dream I can only pray that his soul rest in peace.

***

We bought land about a kilometre from Mangala, near Bandipur. We built a stone cottage and then took a loan to put up twelve rooms on our land. Soon we picked up oxen and a bullock cart, ponies, sheep and dogs. In the process, we were able to help hundreds of tribals who have worked with us and having learnt the basic requirements of urban life, moved on into jobs that have offered them a legitimate source of income away from the forests.

In return, we have been lucky to experience some fantastic and godsent moments in the valley. Life in Mangala has been a roller coaster ride full of terrifying moments and adventures, and continues to be so.

One point that I would like to make is that when I first moved into Mangala, untouchability and casteism was at its worst. I was appalled to learn that when the tribes or scheduled castes walked past the kitchens of high caste houses, the food cooked that day would be thrown out. At some places even the dogs of the household were not allowed to feed on the scraps. The lower caste tribals were not allowed entry into certain homes and had to take their slippers off when they entered others.

When the cottage at Bush Betta was complete, my wife Sangeeta and I invited officials from the administration, tribal leaders and others from the valley, to our new home to eat. It was the first time that people from all castes would meet under the same roof. When I informed all my guests that the cook was from a scheduled caste, there was disbelief, disapproval and even disgust. Many of the invitees decided to boycott the event. Then Mr Shadhakshari Swamy, our Taluk Tehsildar, a person whom we all knew as completely honest, who had worked untiringly for the betterment of all the communities in the area, and whom I had come to respect enormously in all my dealings with him, arrived and dug the first hole for the foundation of the resort that was to come up. My father was there with us as we had our first lunch with the cross section of people from the village. Slowly, the guests began to arrive. We had struck our blow for equality – and today the entire valley knows that class and caste distinctions find no place at Bush Betta, our resort. The flow of guests has not stopped since that first day.

A Difficult Welcome

Master of camouflage and of silent
stalk, the leopard holds sway in the village.

– Murli, tribal leader, Mangala

It was the winter of 1988, soon after Sangeeta and I were married, when for the first time, we stayed on the plot of land where we planned to build our home. Our first accommodation was a thatched lean-to on the upper portion of the land overlooking the serene and sparsely wooded Mangala valley.

We had sunk a borewell about fifty yards downhill of where we were planning to build our stone cottage. The well and the small pump house were just a stone's throw away from our lean-to in which we stayed till the cottage was ready.

Deer, bear and wild dogs would move brazenly around the camp in large numbers, unfazed by our presence. But the elephants were different. Not knowing that habitation had sprung up on the hillside, they would come quite close to our lean-to only to encounter the presence of these strange new animals. Then they would scream and rumble their annoyance. It was almost a year before the crop-raiding herds of pachyderms got used to sharing their space with us.

Apart from the pure thrill that we derived from their frequent visits, we were greatly excited to discover the presence of big cats in the area. A tigress and her family were with us for a short time and, even now, we see tigers from our resort. But what we saw most of, were leopards. They would not only visit but even land up staying with us.

I can still recall the sawing of a leopard, as he walked through our property. I had always believed that predators moved about only during the night, early morning or late evening. How wrong I was. The big cats would wander in and out of the area at any time of the day or night.

The workers would leave by five in the evening, as they lived in Mangala and had to walk home. For fear of elephants, they needed to get back to the village well before dark. After they left, Sangeeta and I would sit on a mat outside our lean-to and await the arrival of the spotted cat. In those heady, early days, it gave us an incredible feeling of achievement and adventure to be living, quite literally, cheek by jowl with wild leopards and tigers. We would sleep in the open, content in the knowledge that if the cats preferred human flesh to their natural prey then by now, surely, they would have killed the many tribals who slept out in their fields each night, protecting their crop and cattle.

Little did we realize then that our relationship with the leopard would cost us dear, and our dealings with the tiger would result in bereavement.

Gundu, our Man Friday, had insisted that we buy two oxen for tilling the land and a cow to give us a daily ration of fresh milk, as we were miles from civilization. He explained that the people of Mangala sell their entire produce of milk to the milk van and there would be nothing left for us. We did as we were told, and bought all three animals. In the six months that it took to build the stone cottage, we were to lose all to the big cat.

The first to go was one of the oxen. It was around two in the afternoon when Gundu had gone to the pump house to switch on the motor to fill the construction tank. April showers had brought the temperature down and that particular day was unusually cloudy, with sporadic rain. Just as he was about to crank the handle of the motor, he heard a funny gurgling sound coming from behind the pump house.

Gundu peeped out of the small meshed window, to find a huge leopard strangling one of the oxen. The cat saw the tribal and glared back at him, growling. With his teeth sunk in the ox's neck, and blood dripping from his mouth, it must have been a pretty fearsome sight. But the lithe tribal had seen it all before and with jungle instinct, he picked up a stone and threw it at the beast. The leopard stood his ground even as the hard-flung rock landed painfully on his head. With his eyes still fixed on Gundu, and his teeth firmly embedded in the ox, the cat shifted its body menacingly towards the tribal, dragging its prey a few feet closer to the pump house.

Gundu kept up the hail of rocks. Each time a stone hit the animal, it would snarl in pain and anger but never did it relax its hold of the bull. It was only when he was sure that the bull was no longer breathing, that the cat dropped its booty and charged at his attacker with fearsome wrath.

The tribal jumped back into the pump house and slammed the flimsy tin door shut even as the leopard slid to a halt just a few feet away. After waiting a while, Gundu opened the door cautiously and looked around for the cat. The big male spotted demon was nowhere in sight and, thinking him to be gone, the tribal decided it was safe to come out. No sooner had he stepped out than he was greeted by another charge. This continued for over half an hour. Just as Gundu was starting to feel that the animal was getting to the end of its tether, and that the next attack might be his last, and just as he was planning to make a break for it, he heard a loud commotion coming from behind. He looked back in shock to see Unni, his wife, brandishing a sickle and screaming at the top of her voice, come charging down from the house to his rescue!

Quite unperturbed by the advancing human, the leopard allowed her to come up to the pump house, before he charged again. This time the charge got the spitting cat to within a few feet of the screeching humans. Just before the cat made contact with Unni, Gundu pulled her into the pump house and banged the door shut. The two stayed put in the security of the small room and not till they heard the leopard dragging the ox down the hill did they head for the cottage.

The leopard had dragged his kill just a hundred feet from the pump house and, for the next two days, both husband and wife watched him eating our ox. Contrary to what we had been told about a leopard's feeding habits, the cat ate through the day and surprisingly, stayed out in the open. Admittedly, it was raining and the sky was overcast with dark clouds throughout the day. We had taken a rented bungalow in Bangalore and Gundu had called home and informed us of the tragedy. By the time I got to Mangala, the carcass had been consumed quite heartily and the remaining portion had been dragged down into the nallah bordering the southern edge of the land.

The success of the first kill emboldened the leopard to kill the remaining ox, in exactly the same place. Yet again Gundu and Unni could do little to frighten him off. Unfortunately, I missed even this episode.

The next time the spotted fiend struck was when I was in

camp. This time the animal killed at night and had dragged our only milk supply, the poor cow, around fifty feet into the bamboo clumps. Word had spread around the village that we had a rifle that could strike at quite some distance without making a noise. Knowing this, one of the tribals came rushing to us and asked me to take the gun and follow him quickly for a terrible evil had seized our cow. I did not have the heart to tell him that there was little I could do with my airgun. Nonetheless I followed him to the spot only to see a leopard straddling the carcass of the cow and staring back at me balefully, his eyes two glowing red orbs in the dark.

I reported all the three kills to the forest office at Bandipur in order to get the requisite compensation for our losses. But knowing the severe financial difficulty that the department had, I did not press home the demand. For the next four years, the cat visited us at least a couple of times a week and when, for some unknown reason, the visits stopped, we found ourselves missing him, despite the losses we had suffered at his hands – or rather, his jaws!

***

It would be unfair for me to end this story without narrating the time when we nearly became cat food. It was the winter of 1991 and the stone house had been built. A few rooms of the resort were also ready. I had work in Bangalore and had gone there by bus, leaving the jeep behind for my mother and Sangeeta and our two young children, Shaaz, who was nearly four, and Zoha who was nearing her second birthday. Not wanting to leave the family alone for long, I decided to get back the same evening, having finished my work by six. I took a bus into Mysore. There had been an accident near Mandya, and our bus reached the old city of Mysore only by midnight. By the time I got connecting transport and arrived in

Gundulpet, it was two in the morning. I knew there was no hope of finding a taxi at that hour, so I walked to Babu's house. Babu is our trusted electrical contractor and I knew I could rely on him for a lift home. I was right. The moment I walked into his home not only was he ready in two minutes flat, but he also had a scrumptious meal on the table.

An hour later we left Gundulpet on his motorcycle. Babu has always been petrified of the forest at night. Earlier, I had thought that this was only because of elephants but on that fateful night, I understood better the reasons for his terror.

There was hardly any traffic on the road at that hour, and we enjoyed the ride, doing good time. We sailed through a deserted Menakemanahalli and then slowed to a crawl as we approached the start of the jungle. Three in the morning is the coldest time of night in the forest. Our hands were frozen, and it was difficult for Babu to use his fingers to de-clutch. When I asked him why we were slowing down, he replied that with the headlights on, riding fast would mean a certain collision with elephants and consequent death by pounding.

Luckily, I was carrying a small torch with which we could just about make out if there were any animals around. Much to Babu's delight, we saw nothing and as we neared Bandipur, his spirits soared and our vehicle picked up speed.

Bandipur just arrives. You hardly even realize that you are about to enter civilization when a blind turn takes you into the forest office camp. Just before you enter Bandipur from Gundulpet, there is a blind S turn and immediately thereafter, you find yourself opposite the reception.

We took the turn at quite a speed when suddenly I found myself thrown against my friend's ample back as he braked hard. Lying across the road, just ahead of us, was a huge leopard, obviously enjoying himself absorbing the heat still retained by the tar. I was awestruck and Babu was dumbstruck. He screeched to a halt and threw himself to the left to get as far away from the big cat as possible. It was a drastic move for we collapsed like a sack of potatoes, the motorcycle on top of us. The leopard knew that the road meant the presence of man, but even he was unprepared for this sudden intrusion into his siesta. He got up in surprise and inquisitively approached the human-machine tangle on the road. I saw him coming and stood still with my torch on him, waiting for Babu to recover. The lights of the motorcycle were on and the engine was still running.

Babu recovered enough to see the approaching animal and lost every ounce of control. Screaming like a lunatic, he decided that running was his best bet. This was inviting disaster, and as he began to run, I grabbed hold of his jacket and yanked him back. The movement threw us both over the motorcycle and closer to the leopard. I hit the contractor hard on the back, shouting at him to shut up and stand still and glare back at the cat.

He was trembling like a leaf and the slap stunned him into submission. Still keeping the torch on the animal I lifted the motorcycle, handed the light to my quaking contractor and with deliberate slowness, mounted the bike. I then asked Babu to hop on. As soon as he was seated, I revved hard and jumped the motorcycle straight at the leopard only to hear a terrified scream followed by a thud as the huge man fell off the fast moving bike. The leopard sprang aside and with tail tucked between his legs, scrambled to the side of the road. I braked hard and did a quick U-turn to pick up my fallen friend.

What I saw chilled me to the bone. The animal was crouching low and getting ready to jump. Just as it was preparing to throw itself onto the cowering contractor, I slammed the bike into first gear and headed straight for the cat. With a funny squeal the leopard jumped back into the bush and stayed there. I collected my friend and drove off in the direction of Gundulpet. I could feel him trembling as he clung on desperately to the motorcycle. After a few hundred yards I turned around and having pacified Babu that all was well, sped homewards to the camp.

Meeting an aggressive leopard on the highway, having him stand his ground and then try and devour Babu, all prove that the jungle and its wild animals are unpredictable. The forest can never be taken lightly. Even though there was a one in a million chance of such an encounter happening, it did happen. And had my nerves, and our luck, not stood us in good stead, it could easily have cost one of us our lives.

Never run from a leopard or a tiger for when you do, you become immediate prey and they follow you out of instinct. It is only after they have killed you that they realize their mistake. Sadly by then it is too late for you. One swipe from a big cat's paw could decapitate you.

This was another lesson that I learnt early in my jungle days. Since this incident, I have been attacked by both leopards and tigers on foot and have managed to stand my ground and call their bluff. That I live to tell the tale must surely prove that so far I have been right.

In the August of 2003, I had a few friends over to stay from the UK. They were the wives of some prospective investors in my wildlife business, and I was hoping for something out of the ordinary to happen to make their visit an unforgettable one.

We were searching for game in the fields of Mangala, and decided to drive to Burrenkatte at night for a picnic dinner. Just after Mangala, I stopped the jeep and got down to check on the tyres. The occupants of the car behind us, friends of ours, called out, 'Careful Saad, a tiger just crossed the road in front of you.' I got back into the jeep to see a leopard that had crossed the road, crouching behind a thorny bush, eyeing a wild boar sow and her litter of four piglets.

Just as she came in range he growled and charged. Within seconds he had pounced on one of the squealing piglets. The moment the sow saw her offspring being attacked, she charged back and hit him hard on the flank. Enraged, she drove him onto a lantana thicket and kept on butting him till he was stuck on top of the bush. She swiped the branches furiously a couple of times with her teeth and then returned to her young.

The mother and the four piglets, one slightly shaken, trotted off into the neighbouring field. The poor leopard scrambled off the bush and managed to regain his dignity before trotting off after them. He was a very large cat and I must admit I was quite surprised at seeing him driven off his food with such ease for he did not even try to fight the sow.

We have had leopards stay in our conference hall, in the thicket of the effluent treatment plant and even in our newly constructed cottages. Our children have had a free run of the place but have never been threatened. In fact, unlike the leopards of Chikmagalur the ones in our area have never posed a danger to humans. I was told that the problem at Chikmagalur started with the custom of certain tribes in the area, of sitting their dead on a wooden platform and leaving them to the open sky. The leopards of the area soon took a liking to human flesh and became maneaters. It was only after a professional shikari had shot quite a few that the menace came to an end. This kind of tradition has never existed with the people of our forests. Wizened leaders like Murli would never allow such an unthinking tradition to be adopted in our jungles.

We are blessed by good fortune that till today we have a female leopard staying with us on our property. She stays in the 'bison cottage' and we allow her complete tenancy rights and full privacy. (In case you want to know why the cottage was called thus, it had nothing to do with gaur or bison. It was because the first manager who stayed there looked like a bison. Yes, she was tall, shiny black, smelled sweet and was powerfully built. She would tower above the entire staff and unfortunately even the management!)

A Tigress Family for Neighbours

Soon will come a day – if the Chinese have their way
When India will lose more than just a tiger a day
Who will hold this forest at bay – If the poacher has his say
And India will lose more than just a tiger a day?
And then ... where will I stay? – To watch the tiger at play
When India will have lost all her tigers one day.

– The author, in memory of a friend

By July 1989, work had started in earnest on the land. The stone cottage was ready, and we had moved in with much joy. We were also planting tree saplings on a war footing. I used to walk around our site every day to check on the progress. It was about five-thirty in the evening, and the workmen had left for the day, when I heard the creature for the first time. A low moaning sound that drifted in with the wind.

I knew the animal was far from the farm for the sound was just about carrying to me, and it was upwind of us as it came from the direction of the Mangala dam which was due west. The moaning roar, for that's how I would describe it, a guttural sound between a roar and a moan, drew nearer and nearer, much to my surprise, as it was not yet dark. I climbed up to the roof of the cottage to try and get a glimpse of the animal if I could.

The road that leads to the Jenu Kuruba village touches the western boundary of our property. The gate was on the north-west corner. I had often walked the jungle path to the dam past a waterhole that was perennially fed by the seepage from the dam and I had, on numerous occasions, seen the pugmarks of a tigress. I had followed the spoor past our farm, down into the nallah at the bottom of our property. Here the spoor would turn left along our barbed fence and proceed for a hundred yards. Then head south and up the opposite hill via the track that could clearly be seen from the stone cottage. She would normally do this at night and very few people living in the valley had actually seen her. The sun sets early in Mangala and even now as I tried to track the sound, it had sunk well behind the hill which is directly behind the dam.

The twilight zone in the jungle is full of music and mystery. You hear sounds of all kinds, insects, birds and animals, which had been silent throughout the day, start their chorus. The mystery comes from not knowing which monster lies behind which bush, the predators hunt during these hours and warning calls of their prey can be heard late into the night. There is nothing more haunting than a tiger's call in the twilight zone.

I could hear the animal coming closer and the nearer it got to our cottage, the softer the moaning became. Finally, from the vantage of my roof, I saw her as she arrived at our gate and turned south onto the track towards the village. What I saw delighted me no end. It was the tigress, and alongside her trotted her three young cubs, just old enough to take an evening stroll with their mother.

She stopped calling the moment she turned south and

then kept her silence till she had reached the base of Kardi Betta, the hill opposite. Then her roaring grew in intensity and when she arrived at the top of the hill, the deep rumbling reverberations rent the night sky asunder. In her wake, she had left a trail of sambar, chital and barking deer honking and barking their warning cries well into the setting darkness.

On following the tracks of the family the next morning, we realized that she had gone straight up the hill and turned right on the path that traverses the hill on top, proceeded to walk along the ridge and stopped for water on the western edge of Kardi Betta. Here there is a small but deep crevice in the rocks that holds water throughout the year. Then she had proceeded down the southern slope of Kardi Betta into a lantana thicket overlooking the Moyar road. In a shallow basin of rain-fed water and thick bamboo clumps amongst a rocky outcrop, she had settled down with the cubs. And there she had remained. A deep growl warned us not to venture closer. We left her there, happy in the knowledge that she had made us her neighbours, as it was obvious that this was where she had decided to make a home for herself and her cubs. It made us feel extremely privileged.

The tigress and her cubs soon became regular visitors to our farm, coming by at least twice a week. This went on for over six months, and in all that time, there was only one occasion when I felt threatened by her.

Knowing that there was a den of wild dogs on the hill, I wanted to find the cave where they littered. I climbed Kardi Betta and having got to the top, started a search of the eastern edge of the hill. Just as I was descending a rock on my way to the cave that I knew was used by wild animals, I heard a low rumbling challenge. I first thought that it was a bear but within moments the rumble changed in tenor and became a warning hiss. Even before I saw her charge, I knew that I had blundered into the tigress. Then she flew across the large rock and came straight for me. In moments like this, as I have said earlier, it is best to stand your ground but this is easier said than done. Nonetheless the one good strength in my character is the ability to control panic under severe duress. I stood my ground and allowed her first charge that had brought her only a few yards from me, to end. Then I slowly started to retreat, step by step, all the while speaking to her in a soothing voice. Standing tall I retraced my steps till I had left the rock. Then came her second and less determined charge. This one I took with ease and kept on my steady retreat proving to her that I meant her no harm. The third charge was barely a shift in her stance and a few steps in my direction. By then I had proven my intentions to her and having satisfied her that I was not a threat to her cubs, started to breathe easy. I walked backwards for maybe a hundred yards and then turning around slowly made a cautious exit from the hill.

Then something happened that shattered our relationship and destroyed my faith in Project Tiger. For it took me a few years to understand that the forest department could have done nothing to prevent what happened – that their hands were tied. Until I grew wiser in the ways of the land, I continued to blame the department for letting the heinous act take place.

One afternoon Nanjundiah, our trusted tribal affectionately called Nanju, called me in Bangalore and reported that a cow had been killed the previous night by a tiger and it was lying on the track that leads to Mangala dam from our farm. Not wanting to lose an opportunity to see a tiger on a kill, I packed my camera bag and dashed off to Bandipur. It takes around five hours to get home from Bangalore and I arrived in the early hours of the evening. Foregoing tea for the excitement of the moment and keeping in view the light that was perfect then, for clouds were closing in fast from the west, we left for the location of the kill.

It was only a ten-minute walk and a strong westerly wind was blowing straight towards us from the thick bamboo thicket in which the kill lay. Nanju walked with care, avoiding twigs and leaves, his eyes scanning the thick bush cover. He would stop every now and then to listen to the various noises, deciphering all kinds of different messages from each movement, sound and smell that came his way. We had just entered a bamboo thicket along the nallah when all of a sudden he froze, a sure sign of impending danger.

Nanju stopped me and said that we had to be careful for he could smell both the carcass and the tiger. I could smell nothing. It was nerve-wracking, for bamboo has a habit of making all kinds of weird groaning and squeaking sounds. To me each sound meant a deadly threat and each squeak would prepare me for immediate flight. Nanju put a comforting hand on my shoulder and cautioned me to be quiet, for danger was around but he knew not what. We arrived at the kill in complete silence. The powerful smell of decaying flesh was strong but the odour of the tiger seemed to be stronger. We could smell the cat but it was nowhere to be seen. I mistook the pungent smell for the territorial markings of a male tiger. Realizing that something was amiss, Nanju motioned to me to climb a tree and keep still as he went further to track the smell.

He must have gone about fifty yards when he called out for me. I saw him collect a few stones and shinny up a thick bamboo stalk. He proceeded to throw these into the bush and make loud noises. He explained later that he could see the tigress but she was not moving. After a stone had landed on the big cat's head and she had remained motionless, he feared the worst and called out for me to come and figure out what we should do. All this had taken till eternity and it was getting dark. The sun had set and the grey jungle fowl had started their piercing calls. These same calls heard from the comfort of a house seem so romantic and quixotic but out in the thick jungle they make your heart race for they signify the onset of darkness and its unknown perils and pitfalls.

I always carry a torch in the jungle, as one never knows when one will need it. Shining the light on the animal, Nanju and I approached the tigress only to see two smaller bundles lying next to her. I knew then that it was our tigress and she was dead. She was lying next to a pool of rainwater, her face contorted in pain with her eyes upturned and a grimacing snarl of death on her frothing lips. I knew straight away that the reason for her death was poisoning as her stomach was bloated and she had been frothing and grimacing in pain even as death had settled upon her and removed her from her misery.

Within minutes we had found the third cub. It was only twenty yards from its mother and had tried to crawl to her and water as his life ebbed away.

Both Nanju and I had a fair idea who was behind the deaths, but we also knew that it would be difficult to prove the crime. The villagers had stuffed the belly of the cow with lethal fertilizer that is so freely available in Gundulpet. The tigress had come back to the kill and fed on the carcass. Her cubs being of the age where they had started eating meat, had shared in the feast with her. She had probably known something was wrong the moment her pains started, and had tried to save her cubs by taking them to water. There she had collapsed with them beside her, and the family had died a miserable and painful death.

Not having a flash in my camera and not wanting to disturb the evidence I went back to the farm only to find that we had no transport to get to Bandipur and the telephone lines were down.

I was devastated for all of us at the farm had grown very attached to the tigress and her cubs. We would even refer to her as our very own family cat. For the first time I noticed tears in Nanju's eyes. He must have seen many an animal being killed and many a tree being felled. To see him in tears showed the depth of the feelings that we had for this tigress family.

Not being able to notify the incident that night, I sent Nanju by the first bus the next morning to report the tragedy to the ranger's office at the Project Tiger headquarters at Bandipur. The rangers arrived in full force and immediately rushed to the spot only to find nothing. There was no cow carcass, no tigress and no cubs. Someone had even tried to scrape the blood away. But they could not hide the telltale signs on the forest floor. The department confirmed our story by reading the signs but could hardly take any action or file a case, as there were no animal bodies to provide conclusive proof.

It was only later that I was told that the family of four felines and the carcass of the cow were thrown into the Moyar gorge at night. The moment the villagers realized that the tigress's body had been discovered, they had removed every piece of evidence to avoid being framed.

Tigers do not respect manmade boundaries and when they come in contact with cattle, for thousands of livestock roam the edges of our forests and national parks, they kill them like they would any normal prey. Carcass poisoning deaths are the biggest worry for Project Tiger and in Bandipur National Park where there was no poaching of tiger, this was the single largest cause of tiger deaths. According to most experts, there is no sure way of preventing the death of the beautiful cat by poisoning, when the death of the cattle itself is not reported.

The then Chief Conservator of Forests (Wildlife) and Chief Wildlife Warden Mr M. K. Appayya had told me that in Bandipur National Park, which is around 864 square kilometres and has a huge common boundary with neighbouring states, with over 2000 elephants and seventy tigers, and not enough staff to protect them, the fight for saving the tiger was a tough one. The department needed help on all fronts, and his belief was that by allowing eco-tourism operators to move into outlying areas, instances like this one would stop.

The Chief Conservator's reasoning was that we would be able to induce the local tribes to respect the wild animals, as the survival of the tiger would ensure a legal and plentiful source of revenue from tourism. He also said that it would be a long and hard battle for us to win. How right and prophetic his words were.

After the death of the tigress, Nanju and I went from village to village, trying to create awareness amongst the people for the urgent need to protect the tiger. We at times even offered to pay the required compensation for cattle that had been killed from our own funds. We explained to them that the benefits of protecting the tiger would only come after we had created confidence amongst the tourists that they would be able to see the big cat in the jungles around Mangala. This way we would get more tourists into the valley and thus would need more rooms at the resort. This would mean more jobs for the people of Mangala.

The Chief Wildlife Warden had tremendous foresight, for after the death of the tigress family there has never been a tiger killed in the Mangala valley again.

An Unpleasant Bully

Treasure the old elephant
for he carries the weight of a thousand souls.

– Old jungle saying in Mangala

The government permissions we needed for taking our vehicles into Bandipur National Park had just come through, and we had worked out the loans for building twelve guest rooms at the farm. In 1989, Rs 18 lakh (1.8 million) seemed like a huge amount of money to me, but Sangeeta said I should take the plunge, and we decided that a life in the bush with the wildlife and tribals as neighbours, was the only way we wanted to go.

The first time I saw him was in the wet season of 1990, whilst I was out on a safari to recce the Burrenkatte valley from the forest side. Work on the resort had started, and we were hoping for a Christmas opening. On the Bandipur-Mangala track just past the eucalyptus plantation, slightly beyond the turn off to the Mangala dam, is a track that turns to the left and proceeds down the valley. A hundred yards to the left is a track made by elephants which leads to a beautiful and serene, perennial waterhole. This is known as Bisonpura and the trail is named after the waterhole, as is the case with quite a few jungle tracks in Bandipur.

The Bisonpura track heads down into the valley and just after a small culvert, which basically is run off from the waterhole, it climbs the opposite hill where it forks, with the left track going across the hill, through some very pretty scrub jungle to Bandipur. The right fork goes along the Dividing Line (hereafter referred to as the D Line) and turns right midway up the hill and proceeds east into the Kathenburra valley. The jungle here is sparse and thins out as it takes the full impact of the people of the Mangala valley. Game abounds in these areas throughout the year.

With the scrub being very rich in protein and the presence of three perennial waterholes, the Bisonpura track is prime territory for big game viewing. Most species of animal existing in Bandipur can be found on this track. Elephants take refuge in the bamboo thickets through the afternoon and after their noon drink at one of the waterholes, wait for night to fall to attack the fields. This they do with gusto for they simply love the ragi that most farmers grow. The sambar, chital, wild boar and sloth bear also head for the fields at night. If one drives along the track in the evening, one can normally see ample wildlife either at one of the waterholes or feeding on the edge of the D Line, ready to launch into the fields as darkness approaches. In the morning, one can view the returning game, heading back into the bush after their night-time raid.

***

It was whilst driving along the Bisonpura track that I first spotted the right-chipped tusker. As we drove down into the culvert, my guide pointed excitedly to the right and whispered 'An'ne.' All I could see was a huge grey rump disappearing into the bamboo thickets to the right, along the stream. This elephant had decided to spend the day in the profuse scrub of the revenue lands before his assault on the tribal fields.

I had started an elephant file and wanted a photo of all the males of the area for the benefit of my guests. Wanting to take a picture of the huge pachyderm, I parked the jeep on the D Line and decided to walk ahead and in front of the animal and take a frontal shot for quick and easy recognition. The tribal guide warned me that the animal was in 'musth' and extremely unpredictable. Knowing that I was not transgressing any rules set out by the forest department, as I would be walking in revenue lands and also that I could control the distance between us and the elephant, owing to the sparse forest cover, I decided to take the risk. For every time one goes into the forests on foot, it is a risk.

The wind direction in the wet season is from west to east and getting ahead of the quarry would mean getting downwind from him. Moreover I was not really worried about the wind in the Mangala valley. In a less sterile environment, this would lead to trouble but here the elephant would be expecting people in the area and thus a 'man' odour should not upset him or so I believed.

I headed further up the track in the jeep and stopped near the fork. Here I got out of the vehicle and cut right in order to get ahead of the bull. I must have gone about 200 yards when all of a sudden I saw terror on the guide's face and before I could ask him the reason, he had disappeared into a deep rut on the side of the road. I looked behind and to my right, and there, in a small clearing above me some thirty yards away, was the elephant, staring down balefully at me with his small, mean eyes.

He was a huge animal and looking at him from the slight depression that I was in, he looked bigger still. I did get time to notice his very large and thick inward bending tusks, and that the right tusk was chipped. As I was trying to get a quick recognition shot with my camera, he charged. It was like standing in front of a steam locomotive. The ground reverberated and the bush seemed to part without any difficulty as he spearheaded in my direction. Forget taking a shot, I dropped my camera and dived straight through the 'wait-a-bit' thorns into the ditch, after my tribal friend.

The elephant must have been ten yards from me when I fell. The fall saved my life, for the rut was a deep gully with sharp banks. It was sheer luck that I did not sprain a muscle or break a bone. I was bruised and bleeding all over, but I barely felt the pain as I lay there looking at the huge tusker hovering above, looking around for me. Realizing that silence and discretion was the better part of valour, I kept as still as possible.

The elephant must have stood on top of the bank for just a few seconds but to me it seemed an eternity. It was only when I heard him walking back through the thicket that I crept back, on trembling knees and a bursting heart, to the Bisonpura track and sheepishly slunk into the jeep.

Did I feel shame as I sat trembling in the jeep? The answer is an emphatic 'no', but I did feel lightheaded in the aftermath of terror. I looked at my guide who had that annoying 'I told you so' expression and told him, in my most authoritative voice, to keep quiet about the incident. I sealed the deal with a wholesome bonus of a hundred rupees. Getting home to Sangeeta and explaining the gashes and bruises was the difficult part. Having experienced elephant terror herself she was paranoid about my frequent stupidity in the jungles and never failed to remind me that we were parents of two young children and should no longer be taking undue risks in the forests. But I was passionate about 'my'

When both the Masai and Samburu fled. Charge at Sweet Waters.

The author—an overnight hero. 113 against the West Indies.

Facing page:
Different strokes for different Nawabs. Mansur Ali Khan, Nawab of Pataudi on donkey back.

Above: *Nanju,my friend, mentor and guide in the forests.*

Left: *Gundu (right) with his elder brother.*

Right: *Murli my friend—the tribal leader.*

She was beautiful —and the wife is not too bad either. Sangeeta with a gaur.

Bandipur is one of the best parks to view wild dogs.

Torn Ears—the magnificent bull who became the most-photographed gaur in Bandipur.

Sangeeta with a leopard cub whose mother had been poisoned and killed.

elephants, and feeling that familiar knot in my stomach for the first time since I had given up cricket, was enough to attract me to every elephant that I saw. That I am alive today is only because I had masters of the forest like Nanju and Gundu to take me through these experiences without any mishap.

***

This was the beginning of a long but turbulent relationship with the right-chipped tusker. There were times when he would corner us and then allow us to slip through by keeping an exit route open, which he could easily have closed with his faster speed through the forests. Of course there were some terrifying moments when he had had enough and wanted to rid this world of pests like us. It is the latter that I would like to narrate here for it does show the unpredictable nature of these great beasts.

I had gone to Bangalore by bus to meet the Chief Wildlife Warden. Having finished my work I took the early morning Ooty bus back to Bandipur. Nanju joined me at Gundulpet with our weekly provisions.

The normal procedure with the provisions was the same then as it is today. Provisions would be purchased at Gundulpet and taken to Bandipur by bus to be kept at the police outpost and fetched on our return from the safari or taken home in the evening bus. This meant that if one came in early, the distance between Bandipur and the farm would have to be covered on foot. If we were lucky, we could take the milk van home. It all depended on when the provisions arrived at the police post.

That day, we reached Gundulpet at noon, having just missed the morning bus into Mangala, and decided to walk home. It was the first week of June, summer had receded and the moist winds had cooled the heat of the afternoon sun. Monsoon showers having drenched the soil, young grass had begun to sprout. It is invariably the Indian gaur (mistakenly called the bison) that move into the grasslands of eastern Bandipur first, followed by the huge herds of elephants. Bull elephants sometimes come in with the gaur and await the arrival of the breeding herds that follow the monsoon rains into Bandipur.

The right-chipped tusker usually arrived around mid May and stayed for five to six months. He had been late in coming this year and we hadn't seen him around. That is, not until the fateful day when we were walking back to the farm from Bandipur. As we ascended the path immediately after the first culvert, not more than 400 yards from the forest office, we saw him standing placidly amongst the bamboo thickets on the left. He must have been more than a hundred yards from the road, far enough for us to make a quick and silent pass. Even from this distance I could see his temporal glands flowing with 'musth'. This is a viscous pungent smelling fluid that flows continuously from the male elephant's temporal glands and indicates to the breeding herd that this male is in the prime of health and the perfect elephant to mate with, for his progeny will be the healthiest of the lot. It is a time when the testosterone level in the animal is at its peak.

During the period of 'musth', all elephants are considered unpredictable and should be deemed to be dangerous. Both Nanju and I had thought that a hundred yards was distance enough for the pachyderm to allow us safe passage. But the right-chipped tusker thought otherwise. We were in line with the elephant, when he charged.

Both of us were surprised by the elephant's behaviour and initially we took the charge to be a mock one, much like the many attacks that we had got used to. But something in Nanju's tribal mind clicked. This something I could not put a finger on for some years, but it was what saved our lives. As the tusker curled his trunk in and made good ground towards us, Nanju took me by the hand and urgently pointed to the drain under the culvert. After a few years in the jungle with the tribals, the first thing you learn is to look for quick getaways from any source of danger.

Elephants have a distance that should be considered their safety zone. Once they break the zone, you run. In a vehicle this is about ten yards but on foot it is seventy yards or so. As the elephant broke this safety barrier, we realized that he was not going to stop.

Quickly we slid down the drain and stood next to the two large drainpipes, ready to go in if required. The elephant was not going to let go this time and descended upon us with surprising agility. Swiftly and without sound we slid into the pipes, only to find to our horror that the elephant had landed next to us with a resounding thump. Perplexed and angered at having lost his quarry he looked around frenetically. Then using his trunk like a snake on the ground he smelt us out. Luckily the culvert was quite wide and the pipes long and we slid easily out of reach. Events were now unfolding at lightning speed and in complete silence.

The elephant knew we were in the drain and did everything in his power to pluck us out. He would rush to the other side of the duct and try and grab us, only to see us slide back and out of reach. This went on for maybe ten or fifteen minutes, after which a resolute right-chipped tusker decided to wait us out and stood silently in the bamboo thicket not more than fifteen yards to the south of the channel. Nanju tried to sneak out from the opposite side only to have the elephant move his position to stand on the road, thus covering both exits. When he decided to feed on the nearby bamboo, we knew we were in for a long wait.

It must have been a good hour later that we heard a large vehicle approaching us from Bandipur. Nanju realized that this was the opportune moment for us to plan a getaway. As the truck neared the culvert and saw the elephant next to the road, it blasted its horn to push him further. Even though there is no need for them to be so, most truck and bus drivers are frightened of elephants.

The bull moved deep into the bamboo thicket and Nanju used the opportunity to jump out of the safety of the pipes and clamber onto the truck. It was an empty manure truck proceeding to Mangala to restock. The fact that the Mangala valley villagers sell their manure to Kerala at a good rate, saved our lives. Having stopped the cumbersome vehicle on the culvert, Nanju gestured to me to slip in. The elephant had somehow known that the arrival of the truck would mean the loss of his quarry and decided, in the usual nonchalant manner so typical of his species, to amble away towards the Bisonpura waterhole.

Later Nanju would tell me that it had been the silence of the attack and a determined gait that he had noticed in the elephant's strides that had worried him. After many years of experience in the bush would I come to recognize and respect these traits!

***

Having told you about the times when the elephant had wanted to kill us, I must narrate an incident which clearly shows that the right-chipped tusker, for reasons known only to him, could be forgiving when he wanted to.

Like most tribals, Gundu and Nanju are hard drinkers. Each evening, having consumed their daily quota, they would walk back from Mangala to their respective homes. One day, when Gundu had had more than his fill, Nanju decided to drop him off home. On the way, who should they meet but the mighty elephant. Instinct is what the tribal survives on in the forest and even in that inebriated state, their sixth sense urged them to depart from the danger area in haste. They decided to run when they could barely walk.

As Gundu took off he fell headlong onto the road and stayed there. The elephant was as alarmed as Nanju when he found one of the puny humans daring to lie down and sleep in front of him. Walking up to Gundu, the tusker gently felt his face with his trunk. Gundu was out for the count and had no idea that an elephant was caressing him. Nanju swears to this day that having smelt the liquor on Gundu's breath, the elephant grimaced and walked back into the bush, shaking his great head from side to side.

Nanju carried Gundu home that evening. The next day found a new hero in the tribal colony. For not many humans have been blessed by an elephant and lived to tell the tale.

In tribal folklore, touching or being touched by a wild elephant is equivalent to being blessed by god. Wanting desperately to be a part of the jungles and the forests I would drive out at night and slap the backs of wild elephants in the hope of being blessed. I would not advise anyone to follow my example, for things can get out of control within seconds. One has to know the temperament of the elephant and the herd, before venturing forth amongst them. It is only after years of studying them and being madly in love with them that I have performed these acts of bravado.

By now I must have been blessed a hundred times, for some mysterious hand has seen me through dangers that most jungle dwellers do not experience, and charges by wild animals that many have failed to return from. I have very rarely been alone during these trying circumstances and have always relied on the experience of my tribal companions to see me through. Call it stupidity or recklessness but there have been instances when I have been feeling depressed and walked into the nearby bush at night. An exhilarating night walk in the jungle is normally enough to cure me of melancholia. But I have always had my tribal with me during these sojourns and that is probably the reason I am still alive.

***

Elephants are the most incredible animals that you will ever get to see in the forests. Observing their social life and intricate bonding behaviour is a must for tourists in the bush. It assures you hours of entertainment and makes you understand that there are other animals in this world, apart from you, that have feelings and a sense of duty. My advice to you whilst out in the bush observing elephants is to follow some very basic rules.

Always remember that an elephant is much faster than you expect him to be. He could run you down faster than you think.

Wild elephants are truly wild and not accustomed to being fed by humans. Giving a coconut to a wild pachyderm could mean your last offering in this world. Many an unknowing tourist has succumbed to elephants that are normally not considered aggressive.

Remember that elephants are very similar to humans in their character. Some are extremely nice and gentle and some aggressive and rude. Every animal, like every different human has its own character.

Never get too close to an elephant wherein you become a threat and remember to stay in your vehicle at all times.

Never throw things at the animal. Never blast your horn, scream, shout or play loud music in the jungle. Apart from disturbing the animals it also agitates them. Would you like it if having troubled a wild animal you move ahead, only to have him pummel the person coming behind you?

When out on a safari always insist that the driver go ahead of the elephant before he stops. This way even if there is a charge, you could simply drive straight ahead and away from danger. But try not to get caught between two elephant herds who are not separated by at least 150 yards. You could become the subject of a pincer attack.

Always go into the forest with experienced and seasoned guides. And always remember the basic rule of the forests. Never panic, normally there will be a way out of even the most difficult of situations.

On foot the rules change and the risks are much greater. Avoid trekking without a very seasoned guide in areas that are known to harbour wild elephants. For he will be the difference between life and death for you, if God forbid, you are ever attacked by pachyderms. Try and keep at least a hundred yards between the elephant and you. Always keep downwind of elephants in areas where human movement in the forest is not expected. If the elephant is moving in an inhabited area, he will not be thrown out of kilter by human odour. But in the deep woods when he is not expecting it, it implies threat.

Elephants like man react to threat in different ways. Some might run away and some might run you down. Try and avoid trekking in elephant areas where man is a rarity. It will help keep you from becoming extinct.

Always, and I repeat always, have an exit plan, by which I mean a quick getaway from the threat. Be it a tree, a culvert, a ditch, rocks or even some odd place where an elephant might find it difficult to get to, always keep an eye open for such areas.

Finally, respect the wilderness. It is awesome and much more powerful than you ever will be. It is wonderful and extremely pleasing to the senses, if done right. But if done wrong then it could be the last thing that you ever do.

The First Safari

The first charge of the elephant will terrify, scare, frighten, and intimidate you. Learn to handle it or ... die.

– Murli, tribal leader, Mangala

Bush Betta opened on the 25th of December 1991 to a full house. On that first day, we drove proudly into Bandipur National Park with our entire contingent of three safari vehicles. We had been driving in the forests for over four years, but had not driven inside the park. To figure out the direction in which each of them should go, the three drivers held a discussion in the dining hall before setting off. Of them, only the old man, Hafeez, had experience with the wildlife of the area within the park. He had retired from the forest department and was responsible for making most of the roads in the tourism zone of the park. In the first few months, I would drive with him and learn the different ways of the jungle from a jeep.

I had decided to take the comfortable Tatamobile, which was completely open to the sky at the back and had a hatch for the people sitting just behind the driver. The Tatamobile is excellent for game viewing as it is sturdy and has a diesel engine that is quite silent. Hafeez had asked me to take the Bolluguda road and then to double back onto the main Chamanaholla track, which cuts through the heart of Bandipur till it touches the Kerala border. The route back from Bolluguda runs along a jungle track that is hardly ever used.

The north-east monsoon having set in, it had rained for a few days and the succulent new grass was emerging, long and fresh. Gaur had arrived with the April showers and were still here in winter, but the elephants had moved on after the monsoons for greener pastures. They would return to catch the grazing of the returning monsoon. The larger herds had not yet reached Bandipur which has open patches of grassland rich in feed. Armed with this knowledge, we departed for the safari.

In my care was an Indian family from the United Kingdom. Anwar and Kiki introduced themselves as avid wild-lifers. Their two children, both girls, sat in the back with the guide, while they sat in front with me.

The Bolluguda road is excellent for sighting tiger and its favourite prey, sambar, gaur and chital, can be seen in large numbers. The route forks twice and if you stay to the right, you can go all the way up to the watchtower.

In those early days in the jungle, I learnt a new lesson every day. I had absolutely no idea then how the animals reacted to different types of vehicles. It was only much later that I learnt that in elephant-infested jungles, silent cars can be dangerous. Because they are so quiet they catch the elephants unawares, and before the herd realizes the presence of the vehicle, it has broken the zone of safety.

Normally an elephant's first charge is a mock one, and is actually a warning telling you to get out of the area. If the elephants hear you coming from afar then by the time you get close to the herd they have already decided their course of action. This could be any one of a number of options. They might run away in panic or silently move away into the bush, stand their ground untroubled by you or start demonstrating their dissatisfaction at your being there. This demonstration can take two forms – threatening displays or actual charges. A threatening display in itself is quite frightening and should be respected at all times. The elephant will shake its head from side to side, stretch its ears out full, squeal, grunt, rumble or even scream. It might even throw its trunk around and take a few menacing steps towards you. It will also kick the ground with its foreleg and dig the grass with its nails. Sometimes the mighty pachyderm will even throw things at you. When a herd is agitated it forms a protective ring around the calves with the younger females, who are by now usually in a state of high excitement, shuffling in nervousness. The herd waits in flustered agitation for the matriarch to decide the course of action that she thinks is best to rid them of the threat.

The matriarch reserves the choice to let the younger elephants remain in their agitated state or pacify them. For her to pacify a younger elephant is quite easy. The older female will speak to the youngster in low rumbles and usually in a tone that is outside our range of hearing. If the youngster does not calm down, she will reach out her trunk and put it in the elephant's mouth. This way she passes on certain hormones to the younger elephant that act as an immediate tranquillizer!

***

On that first day in the park with Kiki and Anwar, we had driven all the way up the hill and spent a few minutes on top absorbing the sight of the undulating green carpet of jungle as it spread for miles under us. We could see the

Blue Mountains to the south and Madhumalai to the south-west.

Having spent a few tranquil moments at Bolluguda we continued with the safari. Coming down the hill, I took the second right and then turned left after a culvert surrounded by a thicket of bamboo.

The path was overgrown with scrub in the initial stages but then it opened up into an incredibly pretty valley with a stream flowing to the left of us. Through the years I have seen tigers relaxing near the water here on many occasions. We crossed the flowing stream as it cut across the track and immediately moved into rich grazing area. Here the road was covered with fresh green grass and I could barely see the track. There was a danger of driving into slush if I missed the road.

Concentrating hard on the track, I saw the elephants quite late. There were only five animals and I could see straight off that they were extremely aggressive. The Tatamobile being half closed, there were certain blind spots to the left. As the elephants were on the blind side, I did not immediately see the charge. It was the screaming of the girls that alerted me to what was happening, and by then the charging group was around twenty-five yards away, and advancing fast. I thought that as long as the herd was behind me I could keep them at a safe distance by controlling my speed. That is exactly what I did, but to my alarm, the elephants kept up the chase instead of veering away.

Anwar and Kiki had by now joined in the chorus and were imploring me to get out of there as fast as possible. I saw the anxious parents in the rear view mirror looking more and more desperate as the elephants closed the gap. Deciding that enough was enough, for the girls in the back were getting pretty hysterical, I floored the accelerator. Just before the rough track meets the main Chamanaholla road, there is a thick clump of bamboo. Here the jungle path takes a blind turn to the left. Driving faster to get the elephants off our back, I took this turn at quite a speed.

A terrifying sight met my eyes. Standing in the middle of the road we were on and blocking the exit to the main safari route, was a mammoth group of over fifty elephants. I had perforce to slow down in order not to panic the herd. The moment I did so, the guide at the back yelled out to inform me that the charging elephants were closing in from behind.

Pandemonium had broken out in the car. The girls hid under the seats in sheer panic, and the guide was screaming at me to go faster, with Anwar and Kiki joining in. Since they were concentrating on the elephants behind us, they had no idea what lay ahead. It was difficult to think logically. I knew we were in a very tight situation. If I allowed the elephants in the back to catch up with us they would smash the rear of the vehicle, thereby killing or injuring the occupants, or they could pluck out one of the passengers with their trunks and finish him or her off at leisure. Or worse still, they could, with complete ease, overturn the vehicle and then polish us off one by one.

On the other hand, if I continued to drive at the speed that I was in, we would upset the herd in front and invite equal danger, as any one of those giants could smash the vehicle in seconds.

Then I suddenly remembered Cynthia Moss's book, *Elephant Memories*. According to Moss, only elephants of the same kin group stay together and socialize. I reckoned that if the elephants behind us were from the same kin group as the ones in front, then surely they should have been socializing together with the huge herd ahead. Why were they not with their own group? Also if they were from the same kin group then they would have warned the herd in front of our approach. That the herd in front had no idea of our presence was apparent from the lack of disturbance within them. This could only mean that the two herds were from different kin groups. That being the case we still had a chance of getting away from the brutes behind us. If I drove into the herd in front without provoking them, then surely the elephants behind us would veer off.

With this in mind I slowed down as I neared the frightening assembly of elephants in front of us. I could see terror on all the faces around me. Anwar and Kiki did not see the elephants in front till we drove into the herd. I had no time to explain my thoughts and just drove straight into the body of animals.

Just as the elephants behind us were about to strike the car, I must have entered the safe distance that different elephant groups keep from each other. They stopped their charge and stood aside as our vehicle disappeared into the mass of grey. The large elephant herd parted with complete ease and as the car drove through, they closed their ranks behind us.

It was only when my passengers realized that we had driven straight through another herd and they saw the clear road ahead, that they started clapping and applauding in the sheer pleasure of being alive.

For a first safari, it couldn't have been a more unforgettable one. Even when I meet the family today, they remember the time when we almost became, quite literally, elephant fodder!

***

Since then, I have seen elephants behave in a way that often defies human logic, and I have come to realize that there is much more going on in the minds of these huge beasts than we can ever imagine. When I read Cynthia Moss's book followed by the volumes written by both Joyce Poole and Lain Douglas Hamilton and applied them in the field, I realized that these animals not only communicate but that they understand orders and have an intricate social system. Dr Sukumar in his books *Elephant Days and Nights* and *The Living Elephants*, has further established that the Indian elephant is as caring and thoughtful as its African cousins.

I do believe that watching elephants socialize is something that every nature lover should cultivate. It really isn't difficult for if you keep your distance and observe them in silence, you will soon learn that they are the most human and gentle creatures in the world. On one of my many sojourns into the jungle with Nanju, I saw a younger elephant go up to a large dominant male and touch his rump to the ground as a sign of submission. He had his tail and ears tucked in tight and reversed into the larger bull with his rump touching the ground. He did this quite a few times till the larger bull reached out with his trunk and caressed him. Then they entwined trunks for a few moments. After that they stayed together for over a month with the big tusker showing great tenderness towards the youngster and the youngster always showing great respect to his elder.

In this case the larger animal was Mr T, a beautiful animal with long straight tusks. He had been shot a few times, once in the leg and once on the body. He had been tranquillized and his wounds treated. Today he is one of the few bulls that have managed to stay alive and can be seen in Bandipur or Madhumalai throughout the year.

Torn Ears and Other Animals

To touch the wilderness once
Is always to carry a part of it with you.

– Peter Pickford

It has been said and proven that elephants over a period of time recognize the vehicle and at times even the people sitting inside, but can the same be said of other animals? I would like to believe that it could. I had a friend, a member of the largest ox family in the world, that allowed me a position of trust wherein he permitted me to become a part of his inner circle. His acceptance of me gave me hours of undiluted pleasure and an insight into his character that I felt privileged to have.

I first came upon him in the January of 1991, grazing next to the Anaikatti waterhole. He looked the same even then. Hugely muscular, shining black, with withering horns and torn ears. The moment I laid eyes on him I knew that the name 'Torn Ears' would stick.

He would come in with the very first showers, just before the large herds, and stay through till December. Come January, he would hop across the state border and head for the hills. He would spend the greater part of the drier months in the pasture and water-rich Sakut plantation, to the east of the Segur Ghat. Segur is the shortcut access to Ooty via Masinagudi.

He preferred to spend most of his time on the 'tiger road' in Bandipur. For that entire season in 1991, I saw him grazing peacefully between Solekatte and Harlikatte. He was one of the few gaur who would leave the comfort of the thick bush well ahead of others. On cloudy days he would stay out in the open throughout the day, and when the sun was shining he would still be out until four in the afternoon. Thus he became the most photographed 'bison' of his time.

Since the days of the Raj, for reasons unknown, the Indian gaur has been referred to in the western world as a bison. This could be because the early Europeans who visited India did not know that there were different subspecies of the genus *Bos* of the family *Bovidae* that existed in the world and decided to call the Indian gaur a bison after the European wisent *(Bison bonasus)* or maybe they mistook the gaur for the American bison *(Bos bison)*. Probably the fact that both the European and the American animals had the terminology 'bison' attached to them was the reason why people coming to India thought that the Indian gaur *(Bos gaurus gaurus)* would also be called by the same name.

In actual fact, the *Bos gaurus* looks nothing like its cousins the *Bos bison* or the *Bison bonasus*. The Indian gaur is one of the most impressive of the wild cattle, with its muscular build and striking light eyes. The bull gaur is massive and at the same time dainty. He stands sixty-four to seventy-two inches high at the shoulder and may grow to over twelve feet in length, including his tail, which could be up to three feet. Recorded weights of bulls shot in the wild go up to 2000 pounds. There is a conspicuous dorsal ridge formed by the extension of the third to the eleventh vertebrae, which terminates abruptly near the middle of the back. A small dewlap hangs below the chin, and a large one drapes down between the forelegs. The heavy horns sweep sideways and upward. The horns of young bulls are smooth, yellow orange in colour and tipped with black, whereas those of old bulls are corrugated, a dull olive in colour and sometimes frayed at the tips. The average horn length is between twenty and thirty inches but sizes of over thirty-one inches have been reported. Cows are much smaller than the males and have slender, more upright and more inward curving horns.

Whenever you approached Torn Ears, he would stand his ground and give you superb opportunities for photography. It is difficult in the Bandipur and Madhumalai jungles to find gaur under good lighting conditions. Torn Ears could always be relied on for incredible shots.

One rainy day when we were driving into Harlikatte, we found him sunk chest deep in a salt lick. For some reason he felt threatened by our approach and tried desperately to pull himself out of the quagmire. It took him a good ten minutes to free himself and saunter off into the thicket. This I believe is one of the reasons for the numerous carcasses of gaur that can be seen littering the jungle floor, having met their end in the jaws of a tiger. Normally, it would be difficult for the big cat to bring down such a large and healthy mammal. But in such a situation, as the heavily built animal tries to free himself, he is exposed to attack and a tiger could then overwhelm him.

Soon after Christmas that year, some of the guests at Bush Betta said they wanted to drive to Madhumalai for tea. It was a cold winter evening, and we donned thick sweaters and stocked the open jeep with blankets before setting off. There is a waterhole just after Bandipur and beyond this point, the road climbs a small gradient. Here it is fenced in on both sides by ten-foot high embankments. As we approached this mound from the north I saw the beam of an oncoming vehicle and slowed down in order for it to pass. What I saw in the beam amazed me.

The approaching headlights were those of a truck slowly grinding its way up, and silhouetted against the light was Torn Ears. As the truck approached the gaur, and the animal realized that all his exit routes were closing fast, he lost his nerve and panicked. He started to dash around all over the place and realizing that the truck was larger than the jeep, came straight for us.

I braked hard and swung the vehicle to the left. The gaur, sensing an exit, went thundering past me and just as he stormed past I leaned across and gave him a loving pat on his rump. The animal threw his head high and crashed into the bush.

For the next three years, we saw the majestic animal almost every day in season, and soon he would allow our jeep to come within touching distance of him. At times he would look up with his huge bulk blocking the jungle track and stand his ground. It was a game he liked to play. If I drove closer he would start shuffling on his feet and skip from one side of the track to the other. If I reversed he would come up to the jeep and perform the same dance. Initially he had me worried for I thought he was going to charge but then over a period of time I understood that he meant no harm. It was just his way of greeting us. On more than one occasion when I came across him feeding next to the main road at night, outside the park, I would allow my hand to stroke the length of his muscular back, as the jeep drove past at slow speed. He never moved away.

Then, after 1998, the great bull seemed to vanish from the park. He may have died of old age or perhaps because his withered horns couldn't stave off the big cats, he was taken by one of them. I shall never know but what I do know is that with his departure we lost an incredibly beautiful animal that somehow knew that the humans loved his every pose.

Both the habitat and the habits of the gaur make censusing difficult. In addition to their extensive travels within the huge conservation area encompassing the Nilgiris, Madhumalai, Wynad, Bandipur and nearby and attached forests, large herds might move across boundaries at a very fast rate.

Physical injuries are conspicuous in the gaur in contrast to most other species that can be observed. I have seen large vertical cuts on the back running all the way down the body. These in most probability would have come from battling with the tiger, the gaur's worst enemy. The frail legs carrying such a huge body are prone to injuries during flight. But the gaur is a hardy animal and is somehow able to survive most injuries.

Apart from the tiger, the biggest threat to the gaur is the terrible rinderpest disease. In the late '60s and early '70s, a rinderpest scourge nearly wiped out the entire population of gaur in Bandipur. That they have recovered speaks volumes for the forest department.

The gaur in Bandipur migrate within the park with a few preferring to head for the coolness of the hills. Inside the park they move either to Moolehole or head for the banks of the Kabini. The others shift base to Madhumalai and even go up the Nilgiri ghats. Gaur have been reported in the Moyar ditch in the drier months. Thus they might even cross the gorge and move south into the Anaikutty jungles and further.

Come the rains, large herds of these beautiful animals trudge back to the fresh grassy meadows of Bandipur.

The lilting song of the male bull in search of females in estrus, that very low moaning resonance drifting through the forest, the sight of the huge animal, jet black and shining stretching his head out and emitting the call to all the females, once heard and seen can never be forgotten.

I have been lucky enough to see the entire mating ritual. The serenading bull, the approach of the cows, the tending period, the flamboyant display by the big brute as he sniffs the females, and the final pairing and mounting. Like the elephant even the male gaur takes most of his weight on his hind legs as he rears up to mount the cow. He is so much larger that the cow is dwarfed under him.

Gaur sightings in the Bandipur tourism zone are excellent between May and January. The bulls can be found dispersed all over, as are the herds. But for photographers the places of interest are Sollekatte, Harlikatte, Ministigutti, Moolapura and Kullukmallekatte. The sighting on and near these routes is tremendous and the animals come out into the grassy meadows even as early as four in the afternoon.

Gaur are shy and retiring animals. But when injured they become as dangerous as the African buffalo. When hunted they are known to double back and become the hunters. To view gaur, approach them slowly and after you have come to within fifty yards, switch off your engine and observe. You are not likely to be disappointed.

***

There are two things that I love to see in the forest. The yellow-orange flame of the tiger as he moves through the bush and the bright flaming yellow of the golden oriole as it flits from tree to tree.

One of the most beautiful sights I have seen in the park is the big male 'Bolluguda' tiger and his mate in consort. In fact, whenever we have seen this handsome creature, he has had a mate in tow. The first time we saw him was when we were coming down Bolluguda with a carful of children. He stood broadside and stared at us for a full minute. With the noise the kids were making, I was surprised that a tiger had stopped for us. But then I saw that he was overtly frisky, bounding from one side of the road to the other. Minutes later we saw the tigress. She was lying flat on her back and taking in the winter sun. Not far from where she was resting was a sambar kill. Then the guide pointed excitedly past the kill and we saw not one but three deer lying uneaten within yards of each other.

When I got back and told Nanju what we had seen he laughed and said that the reason why a mating tiger kills in excess of his immediate requirement is because at no stage of the mating does he want to leave his companion alone. Thus he kills for both of them prior to the act, enough to last them both through the entire mating.

We saw the couple again the very next year but this time they were just off the Kullukmallekatte road. Even with whole groups of screaming children and tourists driving right past them, they would refuse to move.

The best sightings of tiger in the tourism zone of Bandipur are on the Bodhikatte, Bolluguda, tiger road, Moyar, and Bisonpura. The Bolluguda drive is especially scenic as the track climbs up to 4,500 feet.

***

During my breaking in period, when the staff was still assessing my courage and character, I was made to do some pretty foolish deeds. Whenever the elephants would raid us, especially at night, Pradeep, a young Malayali tribal, would come to me and ask if I wanted to go for a walk. He would get all the staff to stand on the roof of one of the cottages so that they could get a good view of us, and then take me straight into the raiding herds. The moment we got into the centre of the group, he would disappear and leave me alone. In those days, the only weapon I carried was a torch, and I would be petrified.

Nonetheless I knew that if I broke and ran or showed signs of panic, I would become an instant joke in the valley. To prove myself, I would have to carry on with the walk and moving straight through the elephants, proceed on my own to the base of Kardi Betta. There I would rest for a minute before starting my climb up the hill. The moment I reached the top and sat down to relax on the rocks overlooking the valley, I would hear the sound of approaching feet. Out of the darkness would come Nanju and Pradeep, bearing a thermos of hot coffee!

It took me two years to prove to the tribals that I was as mad as they were when it came to handling the wildlife of the area.

I love my night trek up the Kardi Betta. The deal here is simple. The right side of the hill is the national park but the left is open for explorations. It is here that I discovered caves with bear and leopard droppings. On these treks, we normally come across elephant and sloth bear. If it is a bear then we make the right kind of noises to ensure that it departs from the area but if the boys come across elephants on the hill, they are ecstatic. Since the hill is very steep in places and offers sheer rock faces, the tribals try and get as close to the lumbering animals as possible. When they get really close, the trick is to keep absolutely still and allow the elephant to pass by at an arm's distance. I must accept that this was one game that I never played. I never did have the guts to get that close to a wild elephant, on foot.

But I must admit I had the last laugh on Pradeep. One of my favourite sports is angling for the Mahseer on the Cauvery. One day whilst out on the river, I asked Pradeep to untangle my line that had been taken by a fish and had got stuck in the centre of the large pool. As he got to the outcrop of rock projecting out of the water, he suddenly realized that it was a crocodile. He screamed out in terror and started a thrashing swim back to the shore. I swam out to him and brought him back, telling him that we were now quits!

That day Pradeep realized that if I asked him to do anything, no matter how daunting the task, he should have complete confidence that I would do it if his courage failed him. I would swim the crocodile-infested waters with my staff. Why me, even my children, Zoha and Shaaz, have spent hours in the Cauvery river with 10-foot crocodiles basking in the sun on the opposite bank!

Ninety-five kilometres south of Bangalore past Kanakapura, I have an angling camp on the Cauvery river called the Great Mahseer Angling Camp. Mahseer, that incredibly powerful carp that can smash a 60-pound monofilament tackle with contemptuous ease, that has been known to drag unwary anglers into the water, the greatest freshwater fighting fish in the world, weighing up to 120 pounds, flourish in the gorge. The Mekhedaatu canyon is proving to be the best place in the world to angle for these giants. The camp is nothing but a few temporary tents pitched in the wilderness with elephants, leopards, sloth bear, spotted deer, sambar, four-horned antelope and barking deer as neighbours. Not to mention the huge mugger crocodiles of the Cauvery which patrol the deeper pools.

Owing to the rocky terrain of the gorge and the extreme power of the fish, whenever an angler is hooked into a 30-pound mahseer, the chances are the line will get snagged on the submerged rocks. Thus it is normal for the ghillie (expert who helps the angler) to swim out and untangle the snag. In the crocodile-infested waters of certain rivers in India like the

Bhima or parts of the Tungabadhra, this would be considered risky but the area that we fish in is so loaded with the natural food of the crocs that till date there has not been an attack on humans. The Cauvery is a killer river and quite a few people die either at Sangam, the confluence of the rivers Arkravati and Cauvery or at Mekhedaatu, a fall where the Cauvery starts its plunge down into the plains of Tamil Nadu. This is either an accident or suicide. There is a belief that when these bodies get washed down the river and end up at Makrimadu, a huge whirlpool after Mekhedaatu, if the crocodiles feed off these carcasses, then maybe they will acquire a taste for human flesh and become maneaters. We have fished out numerous corpses from the river and not a single body till date has been touched by the crocodiles. Thus it is my firm belief that unless the fish population in the region is annihilated, the crocodiles will leave the land-based mammals alone. Left to man and his dynamiting of the rivers for fish, this will soon become a reality in other parts of the river. But the gorge in which we work is well protected from the threat of man and dynamiting and even netting is not permitted in the area thus ensuring a healthy population of fish through the year.

Nonetheless every time that I dive into the Cauvery to free the line, knowing that known man killers thrive therein sends a numbing chill down my spine. Knowing that the risk of becoming crocodile fodder is real, we follow certain set procedures for swimming amongst the crocs.

First and foremost no person with an open wound is allowed to enter the water where the muggers have been sighted. If you do see one, never swim directly at it. This might release a defensive attack and in fifty feet of water that could well mean the end of you. Whilst swimming in these waters where the reptiles associate splashing with humans, for that is the technique the locals use when they swim, it is good practice to follow suit and swim the way the locals do. A graceful Olympiad action might arouse the inquisitiveness of the crocs and encourage them to take a bite off the swimmer just as he has settled into a smooth crawl.

In this part of the river, the crocodiles know that humans do not use the river at night. Thus it is dangerous to swim in the dark for an attack might come because of a mistaken identity. It is also important that the practice of floating dead bodies down the river be stopped. With enough human flesh decaying in the river, it is only a matter of time before the crocs start feeding on it, which could turn them into man-eaters. Lastly, people living in the area should ensure that food waste especially chicken and animal waste, should not be thrown into the river. If the refuse is kept in an open ditch, the birds and the jackals will ensure that it is well harvested.

***

The onset of winter in Mangala was a time when the valley would be filled with the whistling and squealing of wild dogs that would remain with us for the next six months. A fascinating aspect of dog behaviour has been reported by Lt. Col. R.W Burton, who says that dogs – not wild dogs but the ordinary domestic canines – turned loose on the island of Juan Fernandez lost their bark after thirty-three years. But why wild dogs do not bark is anyone's guess.

It is a fact that the wild dog is different from his cousins. They belong to the *genus cuon*. They have more rounded ears, a proportionately shorter muzzle and only two true molars on each side of the jaw instead of three. Because the female might need to feed other cubs the mammae are more numerous, there being usually six or seven pairs instead of the five typical in other canines. The breeding season is from

November to February and the number of young at a birth may vary from two to six or more.

Come December and a pack of fourteen wild dogs would visit the Mangala valley. They would enter the valley north of Kardi Betta, past the Mangala dam, and trot through our farm as they headed up the opposite hill. There they would ensconce themselves in a little cave on the western side of Kardi Betta. It was apparent that the dogs had come to the valley to procreate. This may have been the reason why we could see the female with her pups, both morning and evening, wandering only in the protected area of Kardi Betta, whilst the pack was away hunting. It was as though the dogs had defined an area beyond which she was not supposed to go for the security of the cubs. She never did wander far from the hill and it was only after the pack returned that she would move around.

Every morning on the way out to safari we would see the dogs leaving their den and heading past our land into the jungle. There they would spend the whole day, hunt and return in the evening to regurgitate their food to the waiting pups and the female who had not eaten during the day as she stood guard.

One interesting observation I made about wild dog society was that whereas the cubs fought like mad till they were around seven or eight months old, I never saw the adults fight. I did not quite understand the significance of this, until I read an article on the *Cuon alpinus*. It was their way of choosing a leader. Once chosen, there were no questions asked, for life.

I often came across these beautiful creatures when on foot, and always found them to be exceedingly accommodative of my presence. Walking back from Bandipur to the farm, I have bumped into different packs only to be treated as a friend. I have also seen a pack of wild dogs attack the goats of the village, but only if they happened to be in their direct path – I have never seen these dogs go out of their way to kill cattle or sheep. I agree with Lt. Col. Burton when he writes 'it is fortunate that the attitude of the wild dogs to human beings and domestic animals is almost invariably wholly unaggressive: had it been otherwise, mankind in the forest areas would never have been safe from their attacks.'

For the fact is that wild dogs are arguably the canniest and most intrepid hunters in the jungle. Like their African cousins the dogs hunt in packs and like them they run down their prey but there is a difference. At Bandipur and Madhumalai, the Indian wild dogs do not have the liberty of loping after their prey mile after mile in order to finally run it down as they are hunting in thick bush. Here, in the thick jungles they need to make lightning fast strikes and bring the prey down before it escapes into the thicket. So each hunt (at least those that I have observed) has to be planned in detail. Initially they move around unobtrusively and when they have selected the herd that they intend to attack, surround it in such a manner as to cut off its escape routes. Then a few of the dogs wait at pre-selected spots, while the rest of them attack from an open area from which their approach can be noticed. This not only drives the prey back into the bush but it also panics the herd and as the deer start to flee in terror, the charging dogs guide them into the waiting jaws of their brothers.

An interesting fact that was reported in a study area of forty square kilometres in Bandipur, was that eighty per cent of the kills were attributed to the wild dog, fifteen per cent to leopard and only five per cent to the tiger. Two or three leopards and at least one tigress and a tiger hunted in the area.

The dogs prefer to hunt in the light of day but may do so even in the dark. That is why we must have seen them in the early mornings as they departed for their hunt and then again in the evening, just before it got dark as they returned.

The dogs visited us every year up to 1999, and then stopped. Perhaps it was the electric fences that have come up in the area, or the denudation of the forests on Kardi Betta or the disturbance on the hill – whatever the reason, the dogs just never felt comfortable leaving their pups on the hill again. Sightings of wild dogs used to be really good all the way from Anaikatti to Alchetty. For a few seasons now the dogs have not returned to these areas for an extended stay. The best option nowadays to get a glimpse of these little trotters, as I like to call them, would be to drive along the tiger road.

The realization that we might never see 'White Face' again is sad. This was our name for the most handsome dog in the pack that was whiter than all the others. I hope I am wrong and the pack returns to grace our valley.

***

For the first few years when our land was just an open field, we would only get spotted deer coming in but now that it has grown into a thick bush, sambar seem to have taken over. An adult sambar hind and her newly-born fawn had taken refuge in the lantana thicket next to the waste-water recycling plant. At the same time we had a leopard staying in bison cottage. The worried mother would honk late into the night and from fear of the cat would at times move close to the newly constructed resort rooms. These honking alarm calls have kept many a worried guest locked behind his doors till late into the morning.

The *Cervus unicolor* or the sambar is the largest deer in India with stags standing forty-eight to fifty-six inches high at the shoulder. The length without the tail can be up to seven feet. Weights of up to 776 pounds have been reported in stags shot in the wild, but the average weight of the animal is probably around 430 pounds. The animal changes its colour with the season. Winter is when the colours of most animals deepen and the sambar is no exception. It is an incredible sight to see the beautiful dark brown coat of the stag, sometimes appearing almost black. The average length of the antler is around twenty to thirty-five inches but antlers of fifty inches have been reported.

The inherent ability of the deer to remain inconspicuous makes the exercise of counting them very difficult. Rutting starts from August and goes on all the way into January. The animal is known to lie down in muddy slush and roll. In Madhya Pradesh this is called 'loth'. The English call it wallowing.

This was how the shikaris in days gone by would report the presence of sambar to their rulers. From the jungles the message would go out that 'Sambar loth laga rahe hein' – the sambar are rolling in the mud. The news would excite the princes enough to make them leave whatever affairs of state they were involved in and rush to the site to hunt.

I can recall something similar happening even in my youth, prior to the Wildlife Act of 1972. During the periods when the princes were allowed to shoot a few animals, whenever a member of my family would hear the word 'loth' he or she would drop everything, and rush to the spot. I always found this odd.

The reason why the news would excite poachers who were not allowed to enter the forest in order to get a decent head is quite apparent. During 'loth' the sambar, that is essentially a forest animal, loses its inhibitions and can be tracked with ease, even coming out into the fields. But why it should have this effect on the princes who could enter the forest at will and use their powerful searchlights in the night, is something that I have never been able to fathom. Not enough study has been done to prove that the sambar, like the elephant, are a matriarchal society. Nonetheless, whenever we have seen sambar herds walking on a trail or crossing a meadow, it is always an adult hind (female deer) that is leading the way. A calculated guess would be that like the gaur, it is the sambar male who indicates his preference towards a certain line of action, but the final decision rests with the hind – and it is she who leads the herd.

During our numerous visits into the park we noticed that around the middle of the monsoons – in the latter part of August, and up to the end of November – the sambar started to develop a deep red sore patch on their necks. I have seen the sore resemble a perfectly round red hole like a rifle shot. More often than not the patch seemed to weep. Some experts have suggested that it is a form of weeping eczema while others believe that it is probably caused by the plants and ticks prevalent in the season.

Another theory is that the limited period that the sore appears and its widespread occurrence among the animals suggests that it may be due to a gland; the fact that the sore becomes noticeable at the beginning of the rut when the deer are wandering widely and forming new social groupings indicates that the two phenomena are related.

I would give greater credence to this theory, for there is no doubt that it is just when the sores begin to appear that the sambar start their compulsive roaming, suddenly beginning to wander widely, even at mid-day, and becoming highly conspicuous in sharp contrast to their usual elusiveness. One can find several solitary stags and hinds walking rapidly through the forest, appearing nervous, as if looking for something. It is today commonly believed that this behaviour represents the first stage of the rut. During this time, the sambar move around the forest rubbing their necks on the vegetation as they pass through. Smell plays a major role in the forest in the mating ritual, and this undoubtedly helps in their finding suitable partners.

A large sambar head with a dark shaggy coat is an incredible sight to behold. Sambar sighting is good on the Sollekatte, Harlikatte and Moolapura roads of the Bandipur tourism zone. But the largest herds that I have seen in the south are in Moolehole. For some reason the congregation of the animals here is in huge numbers and it is a fantastic sight to see hundreds of animals thundering across the state highway.

***

Axis axis or the chital are by far the commonest deer found in Bandipur. Their serene faces, their lovely spotted coats, and huge loving eyes endear this species to every tourist coming to the park.

The chital is a medium-sized deer standing about thirty-six to thirty-eight inches high at the shoulder. Its coat is rufous brown and covered with white spots with a dark stripe running down from the nape to the tip of the tail. It weighs between 150 to 180 pounds and the antlers might grow to thirty-nine inches.

In Bandipur, the chital are everywhere and thus become the automatic choice of prey for all predators. The fact that they have been unable to penetrate the evergreen forests is surprising and this may be due to the lack of grazing therein. At night they prefer to come closer to man and civilization as this offers protection from the tiger and wild dogs. Unlike the leopard, which walks straight into camps and villages to take its prey, tiger and wild dog hesitate to enter an inhabited environment.

Chital males can be seen nuzzling and protecting their

harems throughout the year, and every month sees the birth of new fawns, giving rise to the belief that the rutting 'season' for chital lasts the entire twelve months. They are usually seen in the company of monkeys, both langurs and macque. The relationship between the two is symbiotic. While the chital feed on the fruit the simians drop from above, the monkeys also give them advance warning of any predators on the prowl from their treetop lookouts.

There seems to be no fixed leader in chital society. They appear to follow whoever moves first. They have even been seen following larger deer. The group acts as one but it normally takes one in the group to act first.

In the days when shooting was allowed and even till date when poachers brag about their hunts, this beautiful deer is referred to by the rather derogatory term 'bodha janwar', meaning weak animal. In hunting lore, the black buck is the heartiest amongst the smaller game followed by the wild boar, then come the sambar and nilgai (blue bull) and finally the chital. When injured the other animals supposedly run many a mile before falling to the bullet but the chital sits down no matter where it is hit and no matter what it is hit with.

On a misty winter morning, seeing a herd of chital feeding under the flame of the forest as the monkeys above drop down their discards, is a sight to behold. Why people want to shoot this helpless animal is a mystery to me. Yet it remains the favourite prey of poachers and predators alike.

***

Bandipur's deer population also includes the barking deer and the mouse deer. The *Muntiacus muntjac* or the barking deer are often heard in the camp itself, but are not seen in the Mangala valley. They are found in plenty in the surrounding hills. In the Bandipur tourism zone, the best sighting of these graceful animals is along the Sollekatte-Moolapura road.

The *Tragulus meminna* or the mouse deer are very rare and are completely nocturnal. In Bandipur, because our activity is limited to the sunlight hours, we have seen them mainly off the highway, near the fork on the way down to Menakemanahalli. Even then we could see them for the briefest of moments before they crept back into the deep bush.

Of the antelopes in Bandipur, we only have the *Tetracerus quadricornis* or chowsingha, also called the four-horned antelope. This is the only antelope in the world with four independent horns. It is exceedingly shy and prefers to stay in the rocky hills of the Moyar range. I have seen this beautiful light fawn-coloured mammal, slightly taller than a barking deer, even on tiger road but on a regular basis it is found only in the Moyar range. Turn right at the Moolapura waterhole and then turn left skirting Kardi Betta. This road takes you all the way to the Kathenburra stream. Chowsingha can be seen on this route and also on the track to the Rolling Rock Falls. The guides in Bandipur do not know of the existence of this animal and they blindly refer to it as kakkar or barking deer. It is lighter in colour and thinner in structure. It is also faster than the kakkar.

Large numbers of *Sus scrofa* or the wild boar are found in the Mangala valley – and are responsible for such a huge amount of crop destruction that they have recently been given 'pest' status in some states, and can be shot. But be careful when you shoot one, for if you are on foot and the boar charges, it could well be your funeral.

A friend of mine in Tamil Nadu was sitting on the ground in his own farm with a 0.22 bore rifle when in walked a huge boar. He shot at it but did not hit a vital organ and the animal charged. The boar hit him head on, throwing him in the air, and the fellow was lucky to escape being gored.

Another story that goes back years, when killing boar was legal, concerns a Hyderabad hunter. He shot the animal from ten yards with a 12-bore shotgun but the boar took the pellets and ran off into the bush. The person was asked to follow the animal and he, as they say in Africa 'shat in his oondies mon' and flatly refused to do so! On hearing the story I lost complete respect for this supposed great hunter.

The trickiest of animals to handle on foot in the jungles is the *Melursus ursinus* or the sloth bear. Compared to other bears around the world, the sloth bear is medium-sized, weighing around 200 pounds. He has a black, long and shaggy coat with a crescent of white hair on the chest. Although a few of its cousins are adept hunters the sloth bear is a scavenger and apart from its vegetarian diet it mainly thrives on termites. Living amongst them has made us aware of the hazard of having them as neighbours.

The Sloth Bear of Kardi Betta

Beware ... when the black ball comes
for you – you die a horrible death.

– Murli, tribal leader, Mangala

At Bush Betta we get both the south-west and the north-east monsoons and the wet season lasts from April to December. It is an old jungle saying that the rains are a time for great care as this is when bears start their visits.

One of the first lessons that I learnt from the tribes, apart from the danger from elephant, was to be careful of bear. The problem with Bruno is that he is short of sight, hard of hearing and usually has his nose stuffed in some shoot or root. So he is unable to smell you or see you from a distance. Because he does not move away like other animals on your approach, one runs the risk of bumping into him at close quarters while trekking, and then it is mayhem. He could run away in sheer panic or he could attack with the ferocity of a cornered animal. If he decides to run away, you should consider yourself lucky for had he chosen the latter option, he would swipe you with his long talons and rip your stomach open to spill your intestines onto the ground. He could also decide to bite chunks out of your flesh. You would be lucky to come out alive from such an encounter.

In the '80s and '90s there had been quite a few cases of bear mauling in the Mangala valley. We had our fill of encounters at Bush Betta once our small wildlife resort got going. By 1992 we had started to do decent business and would keep running out of rooms for the managers to stay at night. So the bison cottage came to be built, and by June 1992 we had it ready for the young wildlife enthusiasts, who were the only type of manager that we could find to move to Bandipur, especially at the wages we could afford.

It was when this cottage was being built, that a young girl who had gone out to collect firewood near the Kathenburra stream was attacked by a bear and badly bitten on her arms and legs. The second mauling, soon after, was even worse. A villager returning from the fields in the late evening had his guts ripped out and his shoulder mauled. That both persons survived was simply because they had access to transport, which rushed them straight to the Gundulpet hospital. I dread to imagine what would happen in areas where there is no transport available to the locals. There is no doubt that sloth bear can be dangerous. Marga of Aadi, the tribal hamlet next to us had his shoulder ripped apart and Madha, who works for a neighbour, left a chunk of his buttock behind as the bear charged and bit him. Both these incidents occurred within a few hundred yards of our house.

Living in the bush, the staff knew of the dangers of the wildlife with which they shared the land. Every time there was a mauling or killing in the valley, they would light a candle to their gods, to pray for the peaceful passage of the deceased soul. And to thank god that it had not been one of them.

***

We had put up three cottages of two bedrooms each, a swimming pool and a dining hall on 8-foot high stilts on the eastern side of the land. There were six more rooms on the west of the property bordering the road to the tribal village.

Our stone cottage was in the centre of the plot and at the top of the land overlooking the valley. The kitchen which serviced the entire resort was situated in the cottage. The dining hall was about 300 feet away, and the food would be carried across on foot. Lunches were no problem but dinners were always an experience.

In December 1992, one of the boys was carrying out a hot dish of lentils when he found himself in the midst of a silently shuffling elephant herd. He panicked, threw the chaffing dish at the nearest animal and dived into the small bathroom. The poor elephant, not knowing what it had done to deserve being thus scalded, screamed in pain and ran. This caused the entire herd to panic. A panicked elephant herd is most dangerous and frightening. The sounds it makes can be unnerving even for the bravest and most experienced in the bush.

I had been sitting near the pool with a few guests when I heard the commotion. Realizing that somehow an elephant stampede had started, I rushed up to the dining hall only to find a human stampede as well. Guests were jumping off the parapet and running towards the rooms. My pleas asking them to stay in the dining area fell on deaf ears. Luckily the elephants broke the northern fence and escaped into the night but our guests were not that lucky. Some were stuck on the railing having lost their nerve at the last moment, those who had jumped were scratched and bruised and those over sixty who had just sat there and seen the entire episode unfold, were in splits of laughter! Luckily no one was badly hurt and we drove into Gundulpet the next morning to get their injuries treated.

A similar incident barely a few weeks later involved a sloth bear. This time the bearer was Babu, our well-educated waiter from Mysore. It was his first week at the resort and he was carrying our favourite Hyderabadi biryani when a sloth bear suddenly appeared from the south. Babu dropped the rice dish and did the best thing possible against a bear threat. He fainted. The bear ambled away but Babu remained where he was. As he had decided to collapse into the storm drain that runs on the side of the road, it took us quite a while to find out what had happened to our dinner – and Babu. The poor boy was out cold when we finally tracked him down, and we had to revive him with water to get the story out.

The worst incident that I have had with a bear was in the December of 1993. We used to get a lot of foreign inbound groups staying with us. The average age of these guests was about sixty. It was a cold damp evening, having rained heavily. The Bandipur safari into the national park had been cancelled and the guests had made a request for an evening trek. Late evening walks in the forest are fraught with danger. Under normal circumstances one has to be careful and on a damp night when the animals can hardly hear you coming, the situation is riskier still.

Having duly warned our guests and briefed them as thoroughly as we could on how to handle emergencies, we took off. As we trek outside national park limits, I normally carry a 12 bore but that evening, I decided to take my trusted 0.375 H&H Magnum.

We always have one experienced tribal running well ahead of the group who, on sighting danger, signals us to either take a detour, take corrective measures or even return to camp.

Sometimes even the best of trackers can make mistakes and miss an animal – or he could just get unlucky. For at times it does happen that the animal moves into the gap between the tribal and the group behind him, after the tribal has passed. That evening, whether our scout had made a mistake or it was pure bad luck, it nearly led to my being mauled to death.

Heading for the base of Kardi Betta, we had hardly gone a hundred yards from the gate of the resort and were crossing the nallah in the depression just past the south-eastern corner of our fence, when all hell broke loose.

The leading tribal was quite some distance away and had not signalled any danger whatsoever. So it was a nasty surprise to hear the terrifying screech of an attacking sloth bear coming towards us through the thicket to the left of the stream. I knew that this was going to be close for the animal had chosen to attack and not run from well within the danger zone. Why we had broken this zone without seeing the animal was easily explained by the fact that he had been busy feeding along the nallah and must have been moving in a westerly direction along the water course. He arrived at the crossing just as we were jumping across the small stream. The leading tribal had walked past without even hearing or seeing the brute because the bear had not been there when he was crossing. Either that or the bear was moving and had seen the scout coming and stopped to allow him through. He had started to move again after the lead man had departed and moved straight into the group following behind. Having been disturbed once already, he must have been quite annoyed to find another lot of humans marching through his territory. Instead of running he simply chose to attack.

He came fast and he came invisible. One could only hear the thicket parting and the sound of his heavy body pounding the ground. I shoved the guests back and screamed at Nanju to collect them and rush them back towards the resort in one group. The trick in such situations is not to break the group.

Nanju yelled something back which I could not understand and then for some odd reason, kept on screeching like a banshee.

My large torch was slung across my shoulder and I could see the bush parting in the nallah as the bear attacked from the southern bank of the stream. Just as he was about to break cover, I fired the first shot in the air but to no avail and when I saw him burst through the bush I fired the next round, a large and heavy bullet into the ground just in front of his face. The shot smashed into the ground under the beast and threw up a shower of mud and fragmented stone into his eyes. This must have blinded him or he may have been hurt by the flying pebbles; whatever the reason he did an abrupt turn and headed straight back the way he had come. It took mere seconds for the entire episode to unfold and those few moments could have been my last.

I rushed back to the guests to see if everyone was all right. They stood in a huddle, terrified and trembling. They were exhilarated after experiencing the charge, not knowing how close to death they had been but they were too shaken to move and I had to ask for the jeep to be brought to take them back. Nanju refused to look me in the eye. This was a sure sign that he was sulking.

Silently I drove them back to camp, happy that nobody had been injured and content in the knowledge that this story would go into the annals of legend by the time the guests got home.

It was only when we had got back to camp that I asked Nanju what he had been screaming about. Initially he refused to speak to me but then, after a few shots of local brandy had been infused into his ever-willing stout and short frame, he opened up. He said, 'Sar, oof how the bear is the coming that firstly I fully taken aback by sudden charging. When I fully trying to get guests to move back I see that even they are stunned. I desperate and try to prod and push them to get out of danger area. Then mama (a lively plump lady of sixty years) wrapping her arms around me and squeezing like the mighty python. I start the screaming for help but you … you my friend … my sahib refusing to looking in my direction. I then extremely upset with you.'

My old friend Nanju had been annoyed with me because I had chosen to save us from the bear instead of trying to untangle him from the lady's passionate embrace.

Such are the ways of the bush.

Killer

If you don't sleep my child
I will send for the elephant with the single tusk.

– Tribal mother putting her child to sleep, Mangala

He was barely fourteen years old when he arrived in Madhumalai for the first time, alone. This would be the most traumatic year of his life. All his problems had started when for some inexplicable reason his body had started behaving oddly. He felt his muscles start rippling and his lust take on signs that were outwardly quite apparent. And all of a sudden the girls in the herd had started to look at him with a longing that could best be described as reflections of subdued desire. Actually, the apt word would be lust. For unlike earlier when they had hated contact with the scrawny brute, now they would go out of their way to rub shoulders with him.

He had achieved puberty within weeks of his body playing up. And it was then that the matriarch, his aunt, had started to push and prod him away from the herd. She had taken note of the fact that he was becoming unduly anxious to spend time with the young ladies, mostly his cousins, for the herd rarely spent more than a few minutes with elephants that were not related to them. The matriarch could sense that it was time that the youngster went.

One night as the herd was resting next to the Nugu river, she had a quiet talk with her sister. Of late, her sister had become moody and sulky and the matriarch knew that it was the dread of letting her son go that was tearing her apart. But it had to be done. That was the way of her people for if she kept the young adult in the herd he was sure to mate within the group. Both the sisters knew that incest would lead to malformed births and consequent sorrow and pain.

Apart from the mental turmoil of handling a deformed progeny, the whole herd would be at risk if it had to make allowances for an unhealthy calf. Feeding and drinking habits would have to be altered. The greatest risk to the herd would be its inability to move away from danger at the desired speed. The matriarch knew that little things like their inability to travel at a brisk pace through the river that bisects Bandipur into two would make the herd more vulnerable to poachers. For a short distance the Moolehole river forms the natural boundary between Karnataka and Kerala. This is where large numbers of elephants met their end with a poacher's bullet. She did not have to explain the whole rigmarole to her sister for the sister was over thirty years old and knew the ways of the jungle.

The next morning the exercise of seeing off the young male started in earnest. The matriarch would mock charge him and shove him away from the herd. Most youngsters would squeal and cry for sympathy for they would not be able to understand why such harsh treatment was being meted out to them. With tearful eyes, they would look at their mother for support but the lady, who had thundered to their rescue just days ago, would now not even look at them.

Finally the frustration and anger of youth would overcome the insecurity of being without their family and the youngsters would leave to write their own destiny.

Such was not the case with this young elephant. The moment his aunt started her shoving routine, he challenged her front on. Then, pushing her aside, he went to his mother, gave her trunk a last entwine, and left the herd without a backward glance.

That night the elders of the family spoke about the behaviour of the young bull. They shook their heads in anguish, worried about the future of their child. They knew that this young elephant was unlike the rest.

How right they were. As soon as he left the herd, the youngster headed south-east, straight for the foothills of the Blue Mountains. He was heading for the hills because he knew that a few of the old bulls that knew him would be stationed somewhere at the base of the big mountains. And this was a time when he needed friends and advice. He walked with a purposeful stride and after a night's brisk trot; he arrived at the Kakkanhalla stream. Here he rested, feeding on the Napier grass that grew in profusion on the adjoining hill and drinking from the turbid waters of the stream.

It was around four in the afternoon that he ran into a stranger. He knew straightaway that the elephant was not from the area that he had grown up in. He had never seen him and there was something about his attitude that the youngster did not like.

The elephant was truly a stranger to this part of the world. Only sixteen years of age, he had wandered out of the Biligiriranganabetta hills in search of breeding herds that had still not managed to link up with the mighty bulls. He knew that the only available herds would be the migrating ones moving from jungle to jungle for feed and water. He had followed one such group into Bandipur. Having completed his duties and not finding any other receptive females in the area, he had decided to brisk-trot through the Moyar gorge and past the bushy Anaikatti forests into familiar territory.

He had tried to cross the main road near the stream but each time he got near the tar road, vehicles with their horns blasting loudly and people screaming and shouting from within, would block his path. He was still not big enough to worry the vehicle drivers. Some puny humans even got out of large buses with blaring music and threw stones and bottles at him. When he charged them, they ran, only to be replaced by others.

It was no wonder that by the time he came across the younger pachyderm sauntering towards him, the stranger was in an extremely agitated state of mind. Whether he mistook the adolescent's stride for a challenge or it was just the mood he was in, the bigger and larger animal charged the youngster.

The youngster suddenly realized that instead of the friend that he had come to find, a lumbering giant, bigger than him, with aggressive intentions was headed his way. Instinct told him he should run but his mind clouded by anger over the rejection by his family was not ready for another retreat.

He met the larger bull head on and the first impact itself snapped his right tusk from the base. Screaming in agony he wheeled around in order to drive his remaining tusk into the belly of the stranger, only to realize that the older animal was expecting such a move. The stranger side-stepped at the last moment and as he was stumbling past, drove his tusk into the rump of the youngster. Screaming in pain and terror, the youngster turned and bolted towards the hills.

The stranger gave chase but the fleet-footed adolescent,

boosted by the added adrenaline of fear, lost him after a few hundred yards. He forded the Moyar west of Theppakadu and skirting the elephant camp, arrived in the lush valley of Mandradia.

Completely devastated and humiliated, the youngster skulked in the forests while he tried to take stock of his situation and recuperate from his injuries. The open nerve of the tusk was killing him so he chose to eat only the ample graze available without using his tusks. He would cover his rump with mud to stop the flies from sitting on the open gash. His wounds took time to heal but heal they did. It was three months later when he emerged from the forests.

Overly aggressive since birth, the experiences he hadhad since he left his herd had turned the elephant into a thoroughly mean animal. His earlier encounter had taught him not to take out his anger on his elder brethren, so he chose to attack the smaller animals. Cows, buffaloes, deer and other smaller mammals bore the brunt of his attack. Of these, he found the buffaloes the easiest to maim. They would trustingly allow him to come close and then just did not have the speed to get away from his quick and forceful charges. But after killing a few, he lost interest in them, as they never did put up a fight. He needed more stimulation to calm his disturbed mind. Thus he began to terrorize the human traffic in the area with mock charges and threatening displays.

Having learnt the lesson that he should not make contact with anything that was large enough to cause him injury, he would make sure that even when he charged the vehicles he never collided with them.

It was in the May of 1993, during these angry growing up years, that I first saw him on the Masinagudi-Theppakadu road. He was still quite small but the aggression was apparent.

The moment he saw us, he let loose an almighty yell and charged the jeep. Seeing his size I knew he would not hit us. I switched off the engine even as he lumbered towards us. He must have covered the fifty odd yards from where he had begun his attack in a few seconds and before he realized that this particular human was not fleeing, he was onto us.

He applied full brakes and thundered to a halt a few yards away. Then he stood there and shook his head vigorously. Even then the puny human refused to budge. Undaunted, he went back and ripped a sapling – more like a small tree, really – from the roots and hurled it at the vehicle. The jeep remained unfazed. Then he did something very adorable – he ambled up to the jeep and blew us a kiss with puckered lips. The photograph that I have of this is one in a million. After this he ambled off along the Mandradia road.

Each time I saw him thereafter I would shut off the jeep and allow him to complete his full quota of threatening displays before moving on. In this way, a healthy relationship was established between man and vehicle.

***

At the end of that summer, the elephant left the thicker jungles of Madhumalai and wandered into Bandipur. Here he stayed. His beat extended from Menakemanahalli to the Kakkanhalla gate and from the Mangala valley to the Nugu reservoir.

It was in Bandipur in the mid '90s that he killed his first human. Having had his fill of attacking vehicles, his meanness still not abated, he chose to look for humans on foot. The first person to die at his hands was a poor taxi driver.

The vehicles that bring guests into Bandipur usually park near the reception of the camp, which is situated at the entrance to the campus. Just behind the reception are the library and the museum centre. The bathrooms for the staff are also nearby.

It was five in the evening and most department vans at Bandipur had taken their load of guests into the national park for a safari. The taxi drivers would normally get together for a gossip session until their clients returned.

Three of the drivers had just deposited their parties into the five o' clock bus and were heading for the museum centre when they heard a loud trumpeting coming from a hundred yards to their left. Not unduly surprised as camp elephants inhabit the area, they looked up at the source of the sound to see an elephant bearing down on them. It is frightening enough being charged by an elephant in a car but on foot the fright turns to raw terror.

The drivers, however, felt that they were in no real danger as the brute was still over fifty yards away and they only had to get inside the museum a mere five yards from them. But elephants move faster than man can perceive. Even as they were heading into the building, they looked up at the screaming monster to find that he had covered the distance far quicker than they had expected. They entered the museum at a run. It was only when they were inside, that they realized they were only two. They looked back in horror to find that their friend was still outside, on his knees, clutching his heart. At the sight of the elephant coming at them and hearing the terrifying trumpeting, the third driver had had a heart attack and collapsed.

They saw him look up for help and even as he called out to them the single tusker smashed him on the back with his trunk and with a loud crack snapped his backbone in two. The people in the reception heard the bones crack. The poor driver died on the spot. Having killed the man, the elephant kept on running and disappeared past the staff quarters into the jungle.

The second to go was an elderly tribal woman wandering in the bush looking for firewood. She had walked straight into the elephant and he had killed her in exactly the same way. It was not that she was far from her village or that she had not taken the normal precautions that one takes in elephant jungle. She had no idea that he was around for he had waited for her in total silence.

He killed again near Bandipur.

The sudden appearance of forest beggars in Bandipur has always fascinated me. From where they come and where they go remains a mystery till today. At most times there will only be one beggar wandering in the forest all alone. I have never found two forest mendicants at the same time in the same place. Much like bull elephants in 'musth' – for in all my years in the jungles, I have never found two 'musth' elephants together. I have always wondered how these people know when to come and how they get to know that one of their own has died, for they replace him within hours.

This one beggar had been in the area for a few years when one day just past the Bandipur waterhole that lies next to the road, he was gored to death and killed. Nobody saw the animal that killed him but Killer – as the single tusker had come to be known – was around and it was natural that he got the blame for the crime. Killer had another notch on his trunk.

One day driving back from Gundulpet at eight at night, with Nanju and another staff member in tow, I took the left turn from Bandipur towards home and to my complete dismay saw three young men, singing and walking the walk of the drunk, staggering under the streetlight. They were heading in the direction of Mangala. Forest staff quarters can be found constructed regimentally on both sides of the road. To the left live the mahouts and their families and to the right is the school and its administrative staff.

People mistakenly think that this area is safe due to the houses and the presence of the local staff. After a few drinks they decide to explore Bandipur at night and much against the advice of the room boy they take a torch and in their inebriated condition stagger all over camp.

As I got nearer the drunken humans and the beam of my headlight swung full on them, what should I see but Killer, standing just past the glow of the street lamp. And even as I drove up to the group, he charged. Shouting out to my staff to grab the men, I drove the jeep between the elephant and them. Not expecting such aggression from humans, Killer braked to a halt but I knew that he was trying to regroup. I drove the car into him, and it was only after I heard a dull thud that I realized I had driven into his foreleg. He panicked and backed away and then tried to sidestep the jeep.

Meanwhile Nanju had grabbed two of the men and dragged them into the back seat of the jeep and sat on them. The third drunk, not knowing the reason for such nasty behaviour and thinking that we were trying to hurt his friends, grabbed the other tribal and pushed him back. The poor man tripped and fell backwards into a small ditch.

Seeing a human in his direct path, the elephant charged again. I reversed the jeep and this time putting it in four-wheel drive, drove the vehicle into the small ditch that my man had fallen into. Again the elephant balked, as he could not get to his prey. He screamed and wheeled around to get to the poor soul from behind. Sensing his plan, I jumped out of the jeep and pulled the tribal onto the front seat of the jeep.

Yelling at Nanju to grab the third man who was still wandering aimlessly near the jeep, I reversed out of the ditch and started to inch my way back to the main road. Nanju held onto the drunkard and literally dragged him along the road. No sooner had I hit the tar road than Nanju, seeing that the elephant had not followed us, dropped the hapless man on the road and getting down from the jeep, gave him a resounding slap on his face. He screamed at the three men that they could have been killed had the jeep not arrived. They finally understood that they had just escaped death by a whisker. Before they could thank us, we dumped them at the police station and drove off.

The next night returning from a safari, just past the forest boundary, I saw Killer standing with his large rump sticking out onto the road. As he was to my right and as he, like most elephants at night, did not move away from the jeep, I gave his muddy rump an open palm pat. Even this did not move the brute and he remained where he was as we drove homewards.

Elephants seem to think that the darkness of night enshrouds them in a veil of security against humans in vehicles. At night wild elephants are more relaxed and allow vehicles to pass from quite close as they feed on the fresh grass growing on the side of the road. Till date these animals that I have caressed as the jeep drove by, have shown absolutely no reaction to being touched by a human hand, barely seeming to feel my touch. Nonetheless touching wild elephants is highly dangerous and should not be tried unless you are with an expert who knows the extent of liberties that you can take with an elephant or for that matter with any animal. All the animals that I have touched are outside park limits and have never caused any harm or injury to anyone.

***

One encounter with Killer that could have led to tragedy occurred when I was driving back to Bangalore with our two dogs, Tarzan and Chandini. Ramesh our faithful driver was at the wheel and both dogs were sitting at the back of the jeep.

Just as we crossed Bandipur we saw Killer standing to the left of the road. I had my camera, a Canon AE1 with an 80-200 zoom lens, out in a flash. Knowing the animal's temperament and his unwillingness to make contact with cars I thought we were quite safe and asked Ramesh to stop the jeep while I clicked. How wrong I was. I completely forgot that we had two barking dogs visible in the open jeep, and that the elephant would behave differently around them.

The elephant did not charge as was his usual practice but simply strode towards the jeep. This was something new and a worried Ramesh tried to start the vehicle. The unexpected should always be expected in the jungles, the starter cranked but the engine did not fire. He tried again and again but nothing happened.

Meanwhile the dogs had gone wild and were threatening to break their chains and jump from the vehicle. Whether it was to get away from the animal or get him away from us I will never know. Thankfully, the chains held but by then the elephant was right up to the jeep. He tried to put his trunk into the back of the vehicle to pick up the hysterical canines. The elephant was so intent on destroying the dogs that he did not notice Ramesh and I putting our feet on the ground and pushing the jeep. Luckily, we were on a slope and it took only the initial push for the jeep to get into motion. Ramesh allowed it to run a little and then cranked the starter. The engine fired and we were off.

The final run-in with the elephant nearly led to my death. I was returning from Bandipur after a meeting with the forest ranger. It was quite late in the evening and the good ranger had suggested that his vehicle drop me off home. I loved to walk and they all knew it. Thus he did not really press the offer when I declined. I took off at a decent pace. The initial approach into Mangala from Bandipur is at a very slight incline – not strenuous for any walker worth his salt, but enough to prevent you from seeing what is beyond the rise. Just as I had peaked the hill and was passing the eucalyptus plantation, I heard elephants feeding near the Bisonpura waterhole.

I hurried my pace for by now dusk had begun to fall and the last thing that I needed was to bump into an angry elephant in the dark and on foot. I crossed the feeding herd and just as I was nearing the forest checkpost that has a five-foot wall running around the cottage, I heard an almighty trumpet and in that one second that I had to think, the thought flashed through my mind that the tenor had a tinge of frustration and meanness. The next thing I knew I had a charging elephant approaching me from the left.

I had two options. Either to stand my ground and call his bluff or run for the forest checkpost and try and jump the wall before the elephant caught up with me. The checkpost wall was still around forty yards away and I knew I had to make up my mind pretty quickly. I looked at the fast-approaching menace and to my horror realized that I could see only one tusk. The meanness in the trumpeting and the single tusk convinced me that this had to be Killer and trying to call his bluff would be futile. I ran for the checkpost. Killer changed his angle of attack and now tried to cut me off. I knew it was going to be touch and go. Fear gives new strength and terror new speed for my legs flew like they had never done before. Even then it seemed that the elephant was gaining on me and

I would have to think of something else to confuse his small but determined mind.

As I was running I swooped low and picking up a cricket ball sized rock, hurled it on the run at the elephant. Luckily I scored a direct hit for it landed squarely on his forehead. The rock stopped him for the briefest of moments. This respite was all I needed and it was enough for me to get to the checkpost and security. I knew that there was going to no time to go through the gates and I would have to leap frog the wall. I took the rampart with my shoulder going over before the body. I had miscalculated the jump and my left shoulder and ribs scraped hard against the rough wall as I tumbled onto safety. I was hurt and winded but I would live. Killer came right up to the barrier and reached out with his trunk to catch me but by then I had rolled well away from his reach and scrambled into the cottage. Knowing he had lost the race, unlike other elephants that would have milled around in anger and confusion, Killer turned tail and walked straight back to the feeding herd. I waited for the next passing transport heading eastwards. There was no way I was going to walk the forest with this mean animal in the vicinity.

***

I love elephants, and am normally the first to respect their rights and their moods, never forgetting that it is we who are in their domain. But sometimes an animal is born that is treacherous with dangerous intentions. This is the elephant that will go out of his way, come out of the forests, stay in hiding, plan ambushes in order to kill humans. And this animal, I believe, should be put down. Of all the animals I have had the pleasure of observing there has been only one that has, in my opinion, qualified to be in this category. And that was Killer.

So when I got the news that an elephant resembling Killer had been shot by poachers, I felt no remorse. In my view if he had been living anywhere other than India, he would have been shot by the rangers. But the value of life being what it is in India, a disaster is only when a few hundred if not thousand people have died. Just the few deaths that were attributed to Killer were not enough to condemn him.

The Bandipur Elephants

If the elephant vanished the loss to human laughter, wonder and tenderness would be a calamity.

– V.S. Pritchett, reviewing *The Roots of Heaven*

Elephants like Killer were the exception. For the most part, I have found them to be the most sensitive and loving of all animals, and what has really kept me sane in the forests is the time I have spent with them. Hours would turn into days as I followed herd after herd, bull after bull just learning, observing and absorbing as these gentle giants went about their daily chores.

Once we had settled in Mangala, most of the time I spent in their company was filled with joy but every now and then something would happen that would sadden us no end. Acts that to me were cruel and inhuman seemed to give satisfaction to a few perverse and twisted minds. Living in the bush one has to necessarily accept life and death as a hard reality. But even then there are times when the death of an animal that you have known for over fifteen years affects you harshly. My blood still boils each time I think of the unnecessary and cruel death of an old friend, an elephant who we at Bush Betta had named Colonel Hathi. The next story is dedicated to his memory.

Colonel would amble into Bandipur with the April showers. He would stay with us for over six months and having let his 'musth' run its normal course, would sire many an offspring amongst the lush open grass fields of the Bandipur forest.

The first time that I saw him was in 1986 on the Mangala road, feeding in the eucalyptus plantation. He had taken on the colour of the soil and was a ruddy brown mound floating in the tall lantana. His every move was fluid and graceful. The skin on his huge ears, with a prominent horizontal vein running across, had a deep fold back, a sign of achieved maturity. His forehead was a large protruding mass. His tusks were over four feet long, gleaming and perfectly formed. He preferred to use his right tusk at work and when he was not feeding, most times he would rest his trunk on this tusk. It was apparent that soon his tusks would start to cross at the end, and later, if he was allowed to live his full life, they were sure to touch the ground when he lowered his head to feed.

He was not merely big, he was massive. Of late the tribals had reported finding smooth rub marks, ten feet off the ground, on the rough trunks of the matti tree. They said that the circumference of the front foot was over five feet. Jungle lore calculates the height of the elephant by multiplying this circumference by two and the guards placed the animal at well over eleven feet at the shoulder. There was extra weight on the head that forced the nails of the forefeet to dig deeper than normal into the ground. The spoor of the big elephant was distinct.

We saw him every year and I made sure that I spent quite a few days dedicated solely in trying to follow him when he was in Bandipur. The experts put his age in the early forties at the time when we first saw him. We got to know how old he was from Murli, my ancient tribal leader friend. One day after his usual intake of intoxicant's he insisted that he had witnessed the birth of this elephant. The old man loved telling a good yarn, not that I ever complained for I could listen to him forever. Like most other nights, that night too in the December of 1990 we were huddled, around a bonfire in the deep jungles. After having made sure that a lookout was placed away from camp to warn us of approaching danger, we settled down to listen.

'He was born some 490 full moons ago. Not that he could count but in some weird way he, like his species, would be able to put an age to each other,' he began.

'It was a bright moonlit night, I was on a daily wage contract and we were camping at the Rampura forest bungalow with Conservator sahib, when I heard the wailing cry of an elephant in pain. I did not tell anyone and taking my bottle of arrack (a highly potent local brew) with me, I slowly crept to the bank of the river Moolehole. I climbed up a banyan tree and from its branches I witnessed the most incredible sight – the birth of an elephant in the wild.

'The moment I saw the milling herd I knew I was going to see something extraordinary. I peeped between the branches and immediately saw an expectant mother. It was obvious she was nervous. The entire herd was restless, excited, frightened about how and when the baby was going to come. The matriarch, an elderly lady, carefully helped the young mother-to-be up the opposite bank and laid her down on a bed of branches and grass that the herd must have prepared on the soft sands of the river.

'The expectant mother kept putting her trunk in the elderly matriarch's mouth from time to time. Then I had had no idea what that meant but today having worked at Bush Betta, I know that this would comfort and pacify the agitated mother. Every now and then, she would rumble for someone to come and stand next to her. I saw her sobbing in excruciating pain. After five hours of groaning and rumbling, the matriarch, sensing that the time was near, nudged her to push harder. The youngsters in the herd let the old lady do all the work and stood aside to watch, learn and absorb. I knew that the mother was in severe pain but then she was also unlucky that her firstborn had to be such a large calf. The moment the baby's head popped out I knew it was a male. The matriarch helped in pulling it out and gently placed it on the bed of branches.

'Till today I remember how the herd ran, screaming, shouting and raising a din that even my friends at Moolehole said they had heard. The young mother was trembling with the effort. She cleaned the baby and after a short time the matriarch prodded the calf on to its feet.'

With bottle in hand the old tribal went on with great aplomb, 'I swear by the holy spirit even the big bull that happened to be around grunted his approval at seeing the kid.

'Within hours the baby had taken its first wobbly steps and was ready to move. The matriarch realized that there was enough feed in the area for all of the herd and with water nearby, it was an ideal place to settle down for a couple of days. Those were the days when the Moolehole range was safe from poachers and the elephants could stay in the area for long periods of time.

'I was so fascinated that I spent the night on top of the tree, entranced by the loving and tender scene unfolding below me. The kid would suckle on the mother's stomach till one of the elderly pachyderms would come to its help and place its mouth on her nipple. From the very beginning it suckled well. It must have made the loudest noises whilst drinking. The orders of the matriarch were very explicit. Never to let the baby be alone and at the slightest danger the herd would group together and hide it between their legs. That night a pack of wild dogs barged in. This created pandemonium in the herd. The elephants screamed and shouted and milled about in a highly agitated state.'

It was at this stage of the story that we heard the warning whistle from the lookout followed by the snapping of branches by a feeding elephant herd. I had to ask our storyteller to get into the jeep. I put off the fire and with our guests in tow, drove back to camp.

Having heard the story of Colonel Hathi's birth, it was left to me to piece together how he met his end. For today he is no more having succumbed to the bullet. I have tried to put together the sequence of events in the tusker's last days. I have chosen not to take names for I really do not have concrete proof. My story is based on my own observation of the elephant's movements and jungle hearsay. And after having heard the different versions of the people of the area this is what I believe could have happened.

The pre-monsoons in 2001 had been quite heavy and the jungle's rugged brown character had given way to a thick canopy of green as early as April. Where normally he would come around the first week of May this time the tusker had arrived early due to the rain and abundance of fresh feed, and had decided to stop and feed on top of Gopalswamy Betta. That is where he was first seen by Nanju when he was driving up with a few guests who wanted to curry favour with the gods at the Himmavad Betta Shri Gopalswamy Betta temple, high on the hill.

The tusker had stationed himself in the sholas that run down the eastern face of the hill. He would drink from the fresh cool spring water as it trickled down the mountain. He halted here for a few days before descending down into the open grassy meadows of Bandipur. He ambled passed the Bandipur forest department camp and crossed over to the Mangala dam. Here he spent a week and then followed a female in estrus across the road into the fresh grazing of the Kullukmallekatte waterhole.

That month he mated with three females and preferred to stay feeding on the profuse grass growing on the sides of the state highway, the main road that connects Mysore to Ooty and passes through the park, a mere three kilometres from the forest checkpost of Kakkanhalla also the state border between Tamil Nadu and Karnataka.

Vehicles would stop and gaze at him in awe. Colonel Hathi had never minded humans and their childish pranks of teasing or goading him. He would stand his ground and allow the tourists to empty a few rolls of films on him. His composure through it all made me wonder if he had actually started to enjoy the attention that he was getting.

And then one day, late at night, a jeep drove up to him. There was the usual scuffling activity that he had got accustomed to from within the vehicles as the inhabitants prepared their cameras to capture him for posterity.

Then he saw a mean ugly stick being pointed at him and something in his mind warned him that it meant danger. This had not happened before with other vehicles. Colonel had survived to this mature age by following his sixth sense and today it told him that he should run.

Just as he started to move he heard the sharp crack of a high-powered rifle and felt a searing pain rake his right side as the bullet drove deep into his body. In utter confusion, shock and terror, he fled, running as fast as his legs would move. He heard another sound and felt something thump into his rump that drove him onto his knees. Somehow he managed to get up and keep on running. He heard another loud bang followed by a ping as the projectile flew past his ears. He knew that he had been shot but what amazed him was how they had fired in the precincts of this haven known to all his kin as the safe zone within which the elephants could stay.

If only he could read he would have noticed that the vehicle had a Hyderabad registration. Every poacher in Hyderabad knew that number. It belonged to a pleasant-looking man who spoke like a woman and was feared for his dealings with the underworld. This man was known to shoot anything and everything that walked on four legs.

This human was a demented killer and a known evil. He had seen the elephant on a few previous visits and had realized that the animal was perfectly positioned for a quick rifle shot and photograph. With the wind blowing across the road, the chances were that the sound of the gunfire would not carry to the Bandipur forest office and neither would it travel to the forest gate at the border. The photo of him sitting on the big bull, gun in hand would make huge waves in Hyderabad.

On the way in from Bangalore that night, he had found the elephant once again standing next to the road. He had proceeded for two kilometres and having satisfied himself that no forest rangers were patrolling the road, he had returned and shot the animal, firing thrice.

The first shot hit the elephant on the right side of the chest but had gone a mite too low to have hit the heart. The second shot had hit the animal hard on the rump and had driven him down onto his knees. For a moment the poacher had thought that he had broken the backbone of the fleeing elephant and had got down from the jeep to deliver the killing blow. He had been greatly disappointed when the animal had recovered and sped off into the thick jungles. He had fired the last shot in frustration and missed.

On his way back home, as was his usual custom he waved out to one of the young vendors manning the Kakkanhalla gate. The youngster commented as he had done on previous occasions to his friend, 'This jungle is such a lonely place, if only I could get that delicate little hand wrapped around my jonga, I could sleep in peace.' It never even entered the vendor's mind that the fair hand waving out to him belonged to a person of the same sex as him.

Having put substantial distance between himself and the poacher, a badly wounded and bleeding Colonel Hathi decided to head for the safety of the big waterhole that lies next to the Bandipur camp.

The tusker had been shot at around two at night and by the time he limped to Bandipur the sun had risen and the morning light had flooded the waterhole a deep pink. Slowly and with deliberate care, he stepped into the water till it came up to the wound. The bullet had penetrated deep into the body and after having deviated off a rib, had buried itself into his lungs.

Colonel Hathi was finding it difficult to breathe. He looked around him and saw that the large pond had run red with his blood. He felt the calming waters soothe his injuries. He felt so comfortable in the water's embrace that he lay down in the centre of the lagoon.

There he drowned in his own blood and just as his soul departed he remembered his mother's caring embrace as she had left him with the final caution that he should always be careful of man.

That is how the rangers found him the next day. By the time I got there the entire waterhole had turned deep crimson with his blood. The post-mortem showed death by shooting but the bullet was never recovered.

It is a fact that the big tusker was shot on the road and it is a fact that he travelled all the way to the Bandipur waterhole and died of bullet wounds in the pool. It is also a fact that he was burnt and that no bullet was recovered. Without the bullet as proof, who shot him and why will forever remain a mystery. He was not shot for his ivory for there was no way that the poachers could have taken the tusks out in the short span of time that they had between the approach of vehicles on the highway. Thus he had to be shot for some other reason. Even though I have no concrete proof, it is my belief that it was to satisfy a megalomaniac from Hyderabad.

***

When you are the leader of a herd of twenty odd elephants, keeping them healthy and fit is the prime objective. Sounds easy but when each animal consumes around twenty per cent of its body weight whilst feeding and it weighs well over a ton and a half, the amount of food that is required takes on huge proportions.

On numerous occasions I have seen that during seasons of plenty, a whole family of elephants will stay together and the members feed within a few yards from one another. But when the food becomes scarce and the pasture dries up, they split into smaller groups and feed within a radius of a few kilometres, but always within earshot of each other.

I reckon that this is when the young males of the marauding herds learn that feeding over sixteen to seventeen hours in the jungles is equivalent to a quick dash into the neighbouring fields. In the protein rich feed of the fields the herd can consume enough to see them through the day by feeding for around six hours. It is these youngsters who later become problem elephants for people living around the forests.

But feeding in the fields comes with its own risks. Humans are always around screaming, rattling cans and making a huge noise whenever the elephants venture out of the forests. And worse can happen. In June 1992 whilst I was camping on the banks of the Nugu backwaters I saw a sight that would make even strong men cry.

An elephant herd had stopped over in the Nugu sanctuary for a long haul. The family was known to feed in the area for a couple of months. Adjacent to the Nugu reservoir is a trench that was supposed to stop them from getting into the fields. The intelligent elephants must have thought it exceedingly odd that at first the puny humans dressed in green had dug the elephant trench with great effort to keep them away, and then, in places, the villagers had filled it up again for their cattle to cross over into the forest.

One day just as the elephant family was traversing the trench, a young bull of twelve, with an abnormally long pair of tusks, had beaten the rest of his kin to the manmade bridge over the ditch and was moving well ahead of the entire group.

As is the case with most male calves, they show their independence from a very young age. Sometimes even when the family is under threat, these youngsters will be found wandering along the outer perimeter of the herd.

In the forest, the biggest threat to young animals is from the tiger. But a twelve-year-old elephant was far too heavy and powerful for a tiger to overpower and in any case the youngsters made sure that they never wandered beyond the reach of the family in case of any such emergency. Even if a bold tiger did try and bring them down, their screams would have the entire family on the cat before it could do any substantial damage.

But in the fields and in the presence of man, the whole equation changes. Knowing that leaving the immediate vicinity of the herd would spell danger for the young brat, I heard a warning rumble from the matriarch. But the smell of fresh sugarcane was too much for the juvenile and not heeding her caution, he sped on into the lush field.

That was when I heard the loud blast followed by the heart-rending screams of pain from the youngster. From the heaviness of the sound I knew that this was not a rifle shot for that is sharp and normally followed by the thump of the projectile thudding into one of the hunted bodies. Neither was this the sound of the ancient muzzle loaders, guns firing hundreds of nails, ball bearings and sawed off screws and bolts that sting and blind but hardly ever penetrate the skin of the pachyderms, or even the crackers that the people use to frighten off game at night.

All of us who heard the sound, and here I take the liberty to include the young calf's mother, realized with a sinking feeling in our hearts, that this was bad news. The youngster had walked into a country-made bomb. We heard the matriarch ordering the rest of the family back into the bush, as she rushed in with her sister. The two charged to the terrified whimpering youngster who was bleeding profusely. His leg had been reduced to a stump. The charge in the bomb had carried a lethal load and the distraught mother would have known that there was no way that her son was going to survive this ordeal. Seeing the whole drama unfold through my Nikon light-enhancing binoculars, from the vantage of a machan, I knew that he was going to die.

Between the two sisters they managed to carry him back to the trench. There the herd had been waiting anxiously and rushed in to help the youngster over the ditch. They led him to a natural pool, a shallow depression that held water and laid him down.

Nature has a tremendous way of making the ebbing of the soul from the body a painless experience. The youngster was in complete shock and probably could not even feel that his leg was no longer there. By the amount of blood that he was losing he would be dead before the pain set in. That is what happened. Within a few hours of the blast he put his head down on the lantana bedding and slowly succumbed to the injury.

The mother of the dead calf was in shock and in severe distress. Tears streamed down her face, and she refused to leave the youngster's side. She would cuddle him continuously and try and stop the bleeding of his leg by dumping mud on the wound. Her sister let the drama take its course for she knew that the grief of the loss would stay with them till their own death. She went up to her sister and stood shoulder to shoulder with her, not making any sound, just sharing her pain. It was well after the youngster had stopped breathing that she started to bury him. The entire family carried branches and dead wood and buried the adolescent that morning.

I saw through moist eyes, the immediate family going up to the reluctant mother and leading her gently away from the grave. From what I have seen of elephants, it is true that they never forget. I was certain that the herd would come back to the same spot every year and pay its respects to the departed soul. Sure enough, a year later both Nanju and I saw the sisters, caressing the bones and crying whilst the rest of the family paid its tribute to the remains of the young bull who had suffered the ultimate penalty for not listening to his mother's warnings.

***

Given the joy that elephants have brought me, I must end this account of the elephants of Bandipur on a happy note. And some of the happiest times that I have spent were with Jayaprakash.

If you ever happen to come to Bandipur, look around for a shackled elephant with short thick tusks. Do not at any cost approach him without his mahout. He could do anything to you, from cuddling you lovingly with his trunk to pushing you away in anger, not with the intention of hurting you but simply to get you away. Now a powerful push with the million-muscle limb could land you in a shit load of pain.

For at Bandipur we have a marvellous character, a personality that would fit more my actor cousin, Saif Ali Khan than an animal. He goes by the name Jayaprakash. He is the camp elephant at Bandipur, and is beyond question my favourite amongst all the elephants I have encountered. He had been roaming Bandipur well before I got there. He is such a unique character that he has had made every safari into the park in his company an adventure for all who have visited the camp.

Jayaprakash loves to live life to the hilt and hates the chains that shackle him and confine him to camp. He would much rather roam the forests and engage in lighthearted flirtations with his girlfriends, than earn his living carrying backloads of humans around the park. He is by no means a coward and has been known to take on bigger bulls than him, in order to acquire his harem.

Aggressive though he may be when it comes to winning the affections of the fairer of the pachyderm species, Jayaprakash is not at all an ill-tempered animal for he has never gone out of his way to harm humans or any other animals. He has only done what has come to mind. If that has meant breaking his chains and running, then that is what he has done.

One such moment was when clients of ours were sitting on him.

That morning Jayaprakash's mahout had found the elephant further afield than usual from the camp and it had taken time to bring him back for the elephant ride at Bandipur.

When elephants are taken for a ride the mahout unfastens the chains that bind their legs together. These chains are tied onto the animals at night to stop them from wandering far into the forest but allowing them to feed at the same time. The elephants are left out at night to feed and are brought back for work the next morning. The drag marks of the chains help the mahouts follow their spoor.

That unfortunate day in 1995 we had guests from Tanzania. It was like most beautiful November mornings. Dry, bright and cool. There were three of them and all through dinner the night before, they could talk only of the superiority of the African bush and its abundant game. No doubt Africa is splendid and has vast numbers of animals but I have always believed that the experiences that our Indian jungles offer are far more exciting than the staid ones that one normally has in the African bush. A drive into Bandipur is full of encounters and not just sightings alone and this is what makes the Indian jungle so special.

The drive to Bandipur from camp was filled with Tanzanian chatter. We arrived at the forest office to load our guests onto the elephant safari only to be told that Jayaprakash was running late. We walked around the camp premises and I showed them the small museum that we have next to the reception. It was after an hour that the mighty Jayaprakash walked in, ready for the ride. Our guests, who had registered their protest at the delay which would never have happened in Africa, were finally pacified and asked to board the elephant.

Jayaprakash bore them well and ambled on past the reception on his way into the jungle. Just as he entered the bamboo and lantana thicket he went berserk.

It was the time that he had been waiting for. His feet were free from their chains and if only he could rid himself of the chattering humans on his back and make good his escape, he could smash the howdah at leisure in the forest.

With this in mind he headed straight into the thickest of the lantana bushes and the moment he got inside, began what can only be described as a shake dance. His entire body started to quiver and shake from side to side with such gathering momentum that the terrified occupants on his back had to cling to the side of the howdah for dear life. But the shaking and rumbling grew to such an extent that one by one the poor Tanzanians were flung into the bush. The lantana cushioned their fall but the bush being thorny, they were cut all over, before finally landing on terra firma.

It was only because his mahout had jumped off the animal, grabbed his trunk and started talking to him in gentle whispers that the elephant had not run off into the jungles with the clients. The familiar calming voice of the mahout and his own innate desire not to hurt humans, had prevented a great tragedy for if the elephant had decided to run he would have crashed through thick branches and maimed and severely injured the people on his back.

By the time I arrived on the scene, the three Tanzanians were sitting on the ground, stunned by what they had just experienced. I drove them to Gundulpet where we had their wounds treated and then we got back to Bush Betta for lunch.

They never again spoke of how great their Africa was. Jayaprakash had humbled them into silence proving beyond doubt that even our Indian elephants can be as powerful as their African cousins.

That day Jayaprakash snapped his howdah near the Anaikatti waterhole and disappeared for five months. He soon came into 'musth' and moved from herd to herd, mating and siring over a dozen calves. During this period he would not allow anyone to come near and when his mahout tried to get close to him, he turned tail and disappeared into the Anaikatti hills, well past the Moyar. It was after his 'musth' had ceased that he was found again near the Moyar. The whole team of mahouts and a veterinary doctor went from Bandipur to Madhumalai and brought him back without any further incident.

It was said that every time Jayaprakash broke his shackles and ran, it cost the department lakhs of rupees to bring him back. People would camp out in the forest for days, looking for him. Scouts and teams would scour the jungles from Nugu to Annaikutty. They would never find him. It was always Jayaprakash who chose to come back. And come back he did to the people he loved.

Now, he is old and hardly comes into 'musth'. The need to run and mingle with the herds has diminished with age. The graceful elephant roams the camp, preferring humans to the wilderness.

Here I must reveal a secret. In the dry season when there were no elephants in Bandipur, some unscrupulous guides would pass off a glimpse of Jayaprakash as a wild elephant sighting. This is something that both Nanju and I detested and, I am proud to say, never practised.

My children and I have had some wonderful moments with Jayaprakash. He has helped us strengthen our beliefs and has in a way made us better human beings. His spirit and zest for enjoying life even whilst chained has been my greatest learning. The need for space sometimes made him break his bonds but he did so with dignity, never stepping out of line and never harming anybody. All of us have our shackles, and sometimes, the need to break and run gets the better of us. Happiness would be ours, if like the elephant we did not harm any other person whilst breaking free, and made the best of life within our environment, no matter how the cards have been dealt.

The Mangala Tiger

... but the tiger in the wild stands as much chance of survival as an antique building in Hong Kong. I mourn the passing of a beautiful, majestic beast.

– Adam Holland, General Editor, *Asiaweek*, 1993

If I love the elephant then I can best describe my relationship with the tiger as one filled with awe and respect. Living in the forests of Bandipur, I have been lucky enough to observe this incredibly powerful animal in its full splendour, from a jeep, from elephant back, a machan and on foot. Each sighting has only strengthened my belief that the animal, if by some quirk of fate, were human then it would be known as a thorough gentleman.

One such feline that has given me innumerable hours of satisfaction and pleasure was the big Mangala tiger.

The first time I saw him was in 1992 and from then on, I sighted him regularly up to 2002 when he disappeared. On quite a few occasions I have been entranced by the fantastic turn of events that I had been fortunate enough to witness.

It was unlike any other summer day in 1996. There was a distinct aura of tragedy hanging in the air. It was dry and it was hot. The fires had taken their toll on all vegetation. Dust whorls were playing with the trees that stood dry, leafless, waiting … expecting. Termite-riddled logs were scattered in the dusty vastness. The soil was parched, bereft of any water for over two months.

The animals moved with lethargy, every step an effort. Whatever grass remained was withered and brown, low on nutrition and coarse to chew. In the midst of this harshness was a thicket of orange-flowered trees glowing like the flame from whence they got their name. Next to it lay a limpid pool.

The tiger's movements were deliberate. His pale yellow skin, a summer coat, blended superbly with the brown surroundings, the black vertical stripes replicating strands of grass, providing a perfect camouflage. A prominent scar that ran all the way down the right side of his face throbbed with excitement. He crept into place and waited.

The moment I saw the big cat get into a crouch, I knew that it was hunting time. I drove up the hill from where I could see the whole valley including the waterhole and the thicket in which the tiger was lying.

Just three kilometres west of the main Ooty highway, on the road through Bandipur and a hundred yards south of the Kadmathurkere cross cut, the waterhole lay in a shallow depression surrounded on three sides by thick bamboo and a bund or embankment facing the track. The waterhole was not deep enough to meet the needs of elephant herds but was ideal for gaur, spotted deer and sambar. It had shrunk like a naked bladder baked by the sun. The daily trampling of a thousand hooves had churned it into a muddy mass with the drinkable water receding to the middle.

The odour of summer rose from the pool. It was not a pleasant smell, but it was the only source of life-giving liquid for miles. A thick layer of green algae covered the water with dried and decaying leaves floating on it. On both sides of the waterhole were two worn out and heavily used game tracks. Where they met, the slime had parted from the regular disturbance by animals to reveal two oval patches of precious water.

The silence was deathly. Even the flight of the dried leaf could be heard as it broke away from the tree and thudded to the ground. The jungle floor was a carpet of crackling vegetation. The sambar and chital were thirsty and agitated. They knew of the old jungle adage 'one mistake is all it takes, the jungle is never forgiving.' They would look up every now and then to the langurs for any sign of danger, for the go ahead to approach the water.

Even the monkeys were devoid of their usual boisterous play. They hung on the branches, exhausted with the heat. The deer had grouped together at the salt lick and were waiting for one of their own to take the first plunge down towards the water. It was very apparent that not one of them was willing to take the responsibility of testing the waters. After a lot of jostling and stamping, a sambar doe walked purposefully towards the pool. Midway through, she wheeled around and fled straight back to the herd. Youngsters in the herd panicked and ran a few hundred yards back in haste before realizing that no danger was evident. The elders stood still, watching and waiting, ready to flee at the slightest hint of a predator on the prowl.

This was an age-old act that was replayed daily and it was also an old joke that the elders of the deer species sometimes played on the youngsters. It was important for the herd to know if a tiger was waiting to ambush them. If the cat were inexperienced, it would come bounding out of its hiding place after the deer, thinking it had been discovered and fearful of losing its prey. The deer would then bound away, presumably smiling at the cat's foolishness and happy that they had survived the threat of another tiger.

To their relief now, nothing moved and no danger followed the doe. They looked up once again at the langur, which had started to feed and showed no signs of alarm.

The tiger was lying behind a thick lantana bush below the embankment close to where the northern track met the waterhole. He had moved in around noon when there had been no animals around and especially no monkeys to spot him. He was clever. From his hideout, he had seen the entire drama of the monkeys drifting in overhead, the deer getting together, the false approach of the sambar. He had recognized his prey's every mood for he hadn't grown to be eleven feet and four inches from tail to nose in thirteen seasons, without learning a trick or two. Even the hunger pangs in his stomach could not move him to attack a chital that had walked just twenty yards past him. He knew and had learnt the hard way that patience is the virtue of the hunter.

The tiger also knew that before long, the need to drink would outweigh the need for caution, and the herd would move out to the waterhole. After the false departure of the sambar, a big chital stag came next, looked around nervously, saw no cause for alarm, and ploughing through the slush, arrived at the water. Standing knee deep in ooze he started to drink, looking around every few seconds for danger and willing the herd to come. The chital stag needed the rest of the herd to flock in for he knew there was safety in numbers. The wise langur stayed high in the trees, knowing that if there were evil about it would surface now. Nothing happened. Slowly the deer moved in.

The trickle became a rush as the urgent need to quench their thirst soon overcame the herd. The sambar, using their might, for they are the largest deer in India, pushed their way through with ease, till they were sunk deep in the mud. The tiger tensed but still did not move; he was waiting for the herd to fill the retreat paths before he attacked. He waited and allowed even the langur to come down to drink before skirting the lantana in front and throwing himself headlong into the melee of animals. He knew the law of maximum returns, and knowing that he would expend a lot of energy during the attack he needed to drop the largest of the deer. Thus he singled out the adult doe sambar that had played her games with him earlier. She was up front and entrenched in the slush well above her knees.

She tried desperately to push herself back into the fleeing melee and become one with the others. She looked around for an exit but all escapes were shut with hurtling terror stricken bodies and just as she looked back and over her shoulder to assess her situation, even before she could untangle herself from the mud and water, the tiger hit her side on, the momentum lifting them clear off the surface of the slime. And as they were falling, he twisted her neck with a loud crack and she collapsed in the slush with a broken vertebra. She was dead before she hit the water.

She weighed 225 pounds but she was light in the water as he floated her out and then dragged her through the mud and collapsed under the bamboo, exhausted but victorious.

In full view of our prying eyes the big Mangala tiger relaxed on the bund, revelling in the reverberation of the warning cries as the jungle proclaimed him king and the animals scattered in terror. He knew he was the undisputed monarch of this world. He licked the hair off the sambar's rump with his raspy tongue and slowly started to feed.

***

The summer was going to be a bad one. April showers had failed and there had been none of the cloud build-up that normally precedes the monsoons. Towards the end of May when the rains had still not come, the tiger realized that this year was going to spell trouble for the forest. The larger animals that could migrate would do so, including the deer. But the smaller ones would perish. The jungle would become tinder dry and even the smallest of sparks would trigger off a huge forest fire that would kill those that remained behind.

I knew that because the waterholes were drying up he would have to move with the deer. Luckily, his range extended till the Mangala dam but on my last visit I had noticed that even this was drying up.

I also knew that he would make the perennial spring on top of Kardi Betta his base and would use that as his last stand off. Other felines had done just that. The advantage being that even if his regular prey, the deer, did not come, he could kill the underfed cattle of the village and thrive on the drought.

For the moment the tiger was content. The sambar hind would feed him for at least four days. There was enough water to last him for another few hunts. His girlfriend of old, the tigress from the Moyar gorge had started calling. She would be ready for him within a few days and he would go to her the moment he finished his latest meal.

He ate heartily that night and after cleaning himself thoroughly, he slept. Not wanting to shut the access of his prey to the pool, early next morning he dragged the kill further away from the water.

Deer have a short memory. No sooner had he left than the line started to build up again. The tiger looked down from where he lay and revelled in their desperation.

For three days I observed him on the kill and then on the morning of the fourth day, having covered the smelling carcass, I saw him take off for the Moyar valley. Keeping a good hundred yards behind him, I followed him in the jeep. He crossed the highway at the fork and started to call the moment he hit the jungle on the other side. He carried on down to the base of the hill and then having crossed the natural salt licks to his right and walked over the crumbling bridge constructed by humans, he turned left towards Betadekatte, the hill that overlooks the Moolapura waterhole. It was where the track turned right towards the Kathenburra waterfall that I heard the low moaning of his tigress.

She was calling him from the east and he turned onto the Moyar track and proceeded through sparse open bush forest till he came to a bamboo thicket. There he found her next to a shallow depression, surrounded by thick bamboo, which somehow managed to hold water till late summer.

One has to be really lucky to see mating tigers. I have spent years in the bush and have seen this phenomenon as few as six times. The good thing is when they start their mating ritual they seem to do so out in the open, without a care in the world of who is watching. There was a time when on the same waterhole I had driven a bus full of chattering tourists and giggling children, to see the big tiger with his consort on the bund. They had stayed put and carried on with their courtship quite literally as though it were the most natural act in the world!

I was lucky that on this instance I arrived at the very moment that they met. The instant she saw him, she cuddled up to him and started to rub her whole body against his. There were no precursory hellos at this stage. If anything, she was upset that he had come late. She had started calling a few days back and he had not deigned to reply. Not even bothering to explain his late arrival, he mounted her and sank his teeth into the thick folds of her neck. Within seconds of entry he had an immediate orgasm. As his hooked penis ripped her uterus wall on its way out, the pain caused would release her eggs and was excuse enough for her to turn around and give him a hearty open-pawed slap right across his face. He had tried to withdraw but the lithe tigress, that had no other way of showing her pent-up frustration, was too quick for his well-fed body.

He rolled with the slap and slipped away from her for a few minutes of respite. But she would have none of that. She had already lost a day of her estrus and was not prepared to waste any more of her precious eggs because her mate had started to show signs of age.

She sidled into him again and again and rubbed her ripe ovulating posterior on his face. The old tiger grimaced at the smell and desire soon coursed its way into his loins. Displaying the typical feline flehmen behaviour, he prepared to mount her again.

They stayed together on the Moyar road for over three days and in this period, mated at an average of once every ten to fifteen minutes, knowing all the while that I was there and not once showing any signs of discomfort or embarrassment. In the early hours of the fourth morning, the tribals reported that the tiger had drifted towards the Kathenburra stream that forms the eastern edge of the national park. He hadn't eaten anything in three days and was famished after his intense romancing!

The stream had dried up leaving the odd pool. He knelt down in one of these puddles and drank from the black water. Then he walked to the edge of the falls and collapsed on the rock that projects out into the Moyar valley. That was the last time that I ever saw him.

***

What happened next is conjecture. It is again based on the rumours that I have heard in the jungle. The fact is that I never did see this particular tiger again and it is also true that that April night of 2002, the tribals staying in Colony village heard a rifle shot. Colony is a village that was set up by the government for the rehabilitation of the Kuruba tribals.

The full moon painted the gorge in shades of silver. Looking down, the tiger appreciated the beautiful sight of the forest with the thin Moyar river threading its way through. As he lay down he imagined the morning sun painting the valley below in shades of orange, as it slowly flooded the gorge and illuminated the green forest canopy along the small snake-like river which had carved this incredible ravine over millions of years.

The Moyar gorge has been formed by the mighty powers of erosion of the river that begins as Theppakadu and then ends up as the Moyar as it plunges its cool waters into the lower Bhavani Sagar. The Theppekadu originates in Kerala and as it descends to the plateau, it is fed by the spring waters of the Nilgiris, till it becomes a shallow raging stream with numerous pools and rapids. The river manages to hold a variety of fish and till the '60s trout and Mahseer could both be taken from the gorge.

He let the cool breeze rising up from the bottom of the hill caress his whiskers, and enjoyed the rushing winds as the valley maintained its cool temperature even as the plateau above began to heat with the rising sun.

He sat there till the sun's warmth engulfed him and then

he slept. He woke to the sound of cattle as they descended the hill into the stream.

He was ravenous and dying for an easy meal. He just didn't have the heart to run after his usual prey. He turned around and sat facing the sounds of the descending cattle. He knew he was still in the confines of the forest, which was considered to be the safe area for all his kin. The cattle were not supposed to be here but due to the severe drought conditions that persisted in the Mangala valley, the villagers had no choice but to get to whatever available water they could find.

He was not a cattle lifter for he preferred the stringy game meat of the wild animals to the fat-ridden loose flesh of the cattle. He had killed cattle but the kills were few and far between. And he only killed them when they had wandered into his territory. He never ventured out of his domain.

The cows came closer and he allowed one to pass under him before he pounced onto the back of a young female. Already weak from the famine, she brayed her surprise and collapsed under him. He killed her and dragged her back to the rock. Adjacent to the rock projection was a small cave. He was so famished that he started to eat even before the predictable chaos of the cattle stampede had died down. He had his head deep in the cow's stomach and did not see the human face peeping from behind the stunted banyan tree that overlooks the cave.

The cowherd had been appointed by the villagers to take care of all the village cattle during the day. He had risen early for he had to take them far in search of grass and water. He had decided to risk entering the park in order to get to the small pools still left in the Kathenburra stream. He broke the elephant fence near Colony village and managed to cut the sides of the elephant trench to allow his cattle to pass through. Then he stayed in front of the herd as he guided them towards the water. He knew that no forest personnel would be around at this early hour.

He allowed the cattle to descend into the Kathenburra stream and then hung back in case he had to make a run if the cattle were discovered inside the park.

The last thing he expected was the returning stampede. He had heard the strangled cries of one of the cows in distress and had had to move fast to avoid being trampled by the scattering cattle as they charged back in panic.

He allowed them to rush past him and after the last few stragglers had disappeared back towards Colony, he crept ahead till he got to the lip of the gorge. Taking the shelter of the banyan tree, he had peeped down to see a huge tiger stuffing his face with a young cow. He knew that the tiger had not seen him.

Without saying a word about the incident to the villagers, he walked back to the bus stop in silence and took the bus to Bandipur. Instead of reporting the matter to the forest department, he made an out of state call. Even the owner of the telephone booth was surprised when a Tamil Nadu number registered on the phone. The call was made to a person living near Masinagudi.

All the operator heard the tribal say in Tamil was, 'Saar come fast. Meet me at the waterhole, which is just before where the forest ends on the Mangala road. Bring your stick. Come by three in the morning.'

Having completed his call, the tribal paid the operator and took the eleven o' clock bus back to Colony. Then he went to the spot of the tiger kill and prepared a small machan on the banyan tree. The tree was thick with large outstretching branches. Having completed his work in complete silence, he crept back to the elephant trench and gathered all the cows.

Then he went about his day's work as if nothing had happened. When he took the cows back to the village that evening, he said that one of the cows must have got left behind and promised to look for it the next morning.

He woke up at two and walked down the main road to the designated spot where he had asked his friend to come. At three that morning a jeep drove in with its lights out. He jumped into the vehicle and they sped through the sleeping villages. They arrived outside Colony at three-fifteen and parked the vehicle far from the village. Then they walked in complete silence to the machan on the banyan tree.

The tiger had noticed some activity but surmising that it must be a woodcutter, continued to rest and feed in the cave. He was fast asleep as the two humans scaled the bamboo platform.

The false dawn is a phenomenon that has not been explained by science. Birds wake up suddenly, frightened that the morning has past them and maybe they have overslept. Worried that they might miss the first worm they start their early morning routine of rising up. The whole forest wakes up for the briefest of moments and then, realizing that the darkness of night is still upon it, goes back to sleep.

The false dawn woke the tiger and having slept and eaten his fill, he decided to get a drink. He gazed for a few minutes at the beautiful moon flooding the valley then stretching his body, nimbly stepped out of the cave.

The hunter already had his rifle to his shoulder and the moment he saw the tiger silhouetted against the moon, he took careful aim and squeezed the trigger.

There was a deafening roar as the bullet crashed into the tiger's shoulder. His body went numb as his legs gave way and he crumbled. He tried to crawl back to the cave but his limbs were not responding. He tried to call out in frustration but no sound escaped his lips. He lay down on the cool boulder and closed his eyes. And died. The tribal and the hunter threw stones at the cat to make sure that the last breath had left his body, then they quickly scaled down the machan and approached the dead monarch.

The tribal lifted the huge head and placed it in his lap. The hunter took a few photos with his latest Nikon. The flash illuminated the night till the entire reel had run out. Then the hunter took his turn cradling the animal as the tribal finished another reel of film.

Having completed the ritual of photographs the two pushed the body of the tiger over the protruding rock into the valley below. They watched the falling body, illuminated by the pale moonlight, as it tumbled far down into the valley floor.

The hunter slipped his rifle back into its case. The tribal quickly dismantled the machan and threw the remnants down into the gorge after the tiger. He then approached the ledge and pointing the face down into the inky darkness of the Moyar gorge, flashed his torch in a prearranged signal. Back came an answering flash from the valley floor. Satisfied the two trotted back to the jeep.

Yet again, the vendor managing the forest checkpost at Kakkanhalla noticed a jeep drive by at six in the morning. He observed that it had the same Hyderabad number plate and a familiar frail effeminate half-cupped hand waved at him as the vehicle drove past.

***

The tiger in India is being decimated. It is said that at the turn of the century there were over 40,000 tigers in the wild in India. Though there was nothing scientific about the way these figures were arrived at, I believe from reading various authors of that time that there was logic supported by a lot of enthusiasm that was the critical input for calculating issues like numbers of animals in an area. An undisputed fact is that over the short span of a hundred years, this population has fallen drastically. Today, everyone believes that the tiger is in a desperate struggle for survival. And if someone were to ask me how many tigers exist in the wild in India, I would be hard put to find the right answer.

When Project Tiger began, in the early '70s, its first director, K.S. Sankhala derived an estimate of tigers based on his experience. Around the same time J.C.Daniel of the Bombay Natural History Society used a questionnaire survey of forest officers to estimate tiger numbers in India. Both came to the similar conclusion that there were about 2,000 tigers in the wild in the country.

Keeping this as the base, if we were to view the situation after thirty years of Project Tiger, the question to ask is: has it actually saved the tiger and has the tiger population increased due to the project?

I am restricting my answers to my observations in those forests that I travel in frequently. And I would have to say that for me to answer in the affirmative would be a very tough call. My reasons are as follows:

Through the years, tiger sightings have only become poorer and poorer throughout the jungle. I am not speaking about the tourism zone in which we move but the overall park in general. Whenever I passed through Madhumalai, Wynad, Moolehole, Ramapura, Kalkere or Nagarhole, as a member of the Wildlife Advisory Board of Karnataka, I have always enquired about sightings of the big cats in the area. The reported sightings are much less than they used to be. Earlier it would be a difference of a few days when the staff had last seen a tiger but nowadays the answer goes into many weeks and even months. This in no way should be treated as a statement that the numbers have decreased but just an observation that the sightings have decreased.

A prestigious park like Bandipur, which was declared a National Park – Project Tiger well over twenty-five years ago, has never in this entire period got to enjoy the full quota of forest guards that it needed for effective forest management. The reasons for this are diverse and even though this is not the correct forum to address them, the fact is that till the time of writing this book, the forest department has not been sanctioned the requisite funds to fill the vacancies and there is still a huge shortage of forest guards in Bandipur. How the forest department is expected to protect the forests without the essential number of staff and essential funds has always been a mystery to me

The tools used by the staff in the Bandipur National Park are pre-historic. I have travelled all over Africa and wherever there has been a problem with poaching, governments have given their forest rangers the best of fire power and communication tools. Certain areas even have helicopters and planes that assist in the protection of the country's wildlife. In Bandipur, a forester carries a 0.315 rifle and the guards a few old 12-bores. God forbid if they ever get into an encounter with poachers, the poor forest guards would be blown off the face of the earth, before they could even get near their quarry. Added to this, there is a complete lack of intelligence within our forest management system. The anti-poaching squads can never be at all places in the forests at the same time. They have to rely on information, and the network of informers is poor.

Payment of compensation to victims who have lost their cattle to the tiger is another issue that needs to be addressed.

Proper and quicker techniques of diagnosing kills, to enable the department to pay only for those animals killed by the wilderness of the park must be found. The tribal was given a few acres of land and he managed enough money to buy a cow or two. When the tiger kills this animal the tribal is sure to poison the tiger first and then start the process of claiming the compensation. When a tribal moves in the jungle he is bound to come across natural kills of tiger and leopard. A walk in the national park at night for him is no big deal. He will simply slip out of his house with a load of poisonous fertilizer and shove some into the half-eaten kill. Then it would only be a matter of time before the tiger returns to feed and dies. The biggest cause of tiger deaths, in my view, apart from natural causes, is death by poisoning.

Rehabilitation of the tribals next to the forests has resulted in their going back into the bush to make a quick buck through illegal practice. If they really had to be driven out of the forests, then I believe that the tribals should have been relocated near cities and towns and definitely far from the forests. Every time they go back into the forest the conflict with the tiger only increases and it is the tiger that suffers.

I have worked with over 500 tribals and till date no convincing explanation, apart from making money through tourism, has been given to them as to why they need to save the tiger and the wildlife of the area. Perhaps it is time that we started this process of helping them understand the ecological as well as the commercial reasons for saving the tiger.

So today do I believe that the tiger has recovered and increased its numbers from the 2,000 that was predicted in 1972? My answer is a sad negative. I would be happy just to know that the figure has not dropped well below the original estimate of 2,000.

Were the nawabs and rajas better conservationists? Were the British more proficient at protecting our wildlife? The answer is a bit of both. I think both the British and the royalty did a lot to establish conservation and protection norms for wildlife. If you were to ask me if they did more than the government of independent India, then knowing that they believed in hunting for pleasure, I would be hard pressed to find the correct answer for I do not have access to wildlife statistics during the Raj. It is not that their pleasure knew no bounds, they had ample fund allocation for conservation and by the 1880s even had a firm conservation policy but I do not believe that they had mastered the expertise to work out an optimum carrying capacity for their forests.

All I can say is that the rulers and their nobility fiercely and jealously guarded their wildlife and jungles. This I know for a fact is untrue of the forest managers of today.

Snakes and Other Anecdotes

Keep your hands inside the blanket as you sleep the night away. For the darkness belongs to the krait.

– Unni, Gundu's wife, Bush Betta camp

One of my earlier fears in the bush was the threat of snakebite. Surprisingly, we have hardly ever had a problem with reptiles. We have come across numerous species but they have preferred to move out of the way and chosen not to make contact.

The only time when we have been hit was on a night trek. When walking in the dark, I am doubly careful about the safety rules that need to be followed. I insist that the group wear trousers and walking shoes and always carry a torch. This is apart from the regular safety drill that I insist upon. Such as walking in single file, avoiding stepping on crackling and noisy branches and leaves, avoiding overhanging branches from fear of the saw-scaled vipers and listening to every sound that the forest makes and understanding every clue that comes our way for it is only by being careful and knowing the bush, that one can survive it. Our visitors follow what I say because they believe that I am speaking through experience. But the

Prophet is rarely honoured in his own land. One's own son has to rebel against what the father says and more often than not comes a cropper. That is exactly what happened to Shaaz.

It was in 2001, the monsoons had just ended and the ground was covered with a six-inch deep fall of moist and rotting leaves. Shaaz, then aged twelve, and I had taken a group of guests for a barbecue out in the bush. Having finished dinner, the guests expressed a desire to go on a night trek. We took off in a group of five with Shaaz just behind me. I was behind the leading scout who had gone ahead to see the cause of the noise that we had heard in the jungle whilst we were eating. We could hear elephant in the distance and had our ears and eyes open for signs of danger.

The thick layer of leaves that covered the ground was ideal habitat for reptiles which was why I had chosen to walk in front. We crossed the nallah on the way to the tribal village through the bamboo jungle. We had just set foot on the leaf-strewn path when I heard my son wince and then the sound of something small slithering away. I asked Shaaz if he was all right and he said that something had stung him on his foot. I shone the torch on his left leg and was horrified to see that he was wearing open sandals and between the straps on his skin were two identical puncture marks. They were small and bleeding. In order not to frighten the child and terrify the guests, I said that it was a large ant bite.

Using the close proximity of the elephants as an excuse to terminate the trek, I returned to camp. There I inspected Shaaz's foot more closely, and realized that there was no local symptom. This worried me for the only poisonous snake that bites and leaves no early symptoms is the krait. It is also the largest killer of humans in our part of the jungles. How this happens is quite frightening. People in the villages are quite susceptible to snakebite at night. In summer they sleep out in the open or in their veranda or terrace and in the monsoons and winter they move into the relative warmth of their homes.

Most houses in the villages are poorly built with many gaps and crevices in the structure. Snakes can be found in these cracks in the woodwork and at times in the walls themselves. The place that guarantees a snake in the house is the crevice that is formed where the roof rests on the wall. Rats relish these areas of comfort and infest these homes. Snakes come looking for rats and find their way into the house with comparative ease. Some might come and go but many prefer to settle down in the clefts. A spring-cleaning of our stone cottage would always yield a few shed skins. Sleeping people at night tend to shift around. A flung arm or a shifting leg might just land on a hunting snake. It will bite in a defensive reaction and not because it has gone out of its way to find a human to kill.

If the snake happens to be a cobra or a viper, the pain is immediate, and acute enough to awaken the person. This gives him enough time to take corrective action before the venom floods the system. But if the snake is a krait then the victim will most surely perish unless he is disturbed enough by the sounds made by the reptile and actually sees it next to him. The krait has very small fangs with which it delivers its lethal dose of neuro toxins. Because of the size of the fangs and because there are hardly any painful symptoms from a krait bite in the initial stages when the toxin is spreading, the sleeping victim more often than not continues to sleep until he starts suffering from a feeling of suffocation. By this time, the poison has usually spread sufficiently to start shutting down the nervous system, and death is a few minutes away.

That is why when Shaaz showed no external signs of poisoning, I panicked. I called the local hospital in Gundulpet and they confirmed that they had the required anti-venom.

We drove into the hospital and found to our relief that a snake had bitten the heir apparent but no poison had been injected. This was either because the snake itself was a non-poisonous one or it was one with poison but had delivered a 'dry' bite.

Yes, snakes do bite and at times do not release their venom. I only learned this when I read Romulus Whitaker's book on Indian snakes. He goes on to explain that only twenty-five per cent of snakes in India are poisonous and about fifty per cent of the time the venomous snake does not release its poison. This means that of all the snakebites in India only around twelve per cent actually have venom injected.

What I find fascinating in the jungles is why something happens to one person but not to the one closest to him. I was walking ahead of my son and the snake had avoided striking me but had sunk its fangs into him. I was the one who must have trodden on him first. This is the way of the jungle. Animals are wild and nothing can ever be predicted. The one immutable law of the jungle is that whenever you enter it, you should be ready for anything, most of all death.

***

When we had started work on our site, the snake that we disturbed the most was the green kukri. No sooner had the work started than these snakes disappeared. Others remained and can be seen even today but for reasons that I cannot fathom, the kukri chose to desert the area.

The scariest incident with a reptile took place on the sand road of Madhumalai Sanctuary. In the '80s one was allowed to take private vehicles into the sanctuary. I was driving the Tatamobile with Nanju sitting at the back. It was around five in the evening when I saw a python crossing the road. I approached the slowly moving snake with care. As I came abreast of the reptile and no sooner had I taken out my camera than the huge serpent flared up and charged the vehicle. Even though we were safely inside a car, both Nanju and I were shocked at seeing a 12-foot snake bearing down at us. I had just managed a quick shot with my Canon AE1 when I heard Nanju screaming. The snake had risen off the ground and smashed the glass of the window behind me, spraying the glass with saliva. Throwing the camera to one side, I released the clutch and we drove off as fast as the Tatamobile could go!

On yet another wet and cold afternoon we had a full house of guests checking in at Bush Betta. I had been deputed to take the clients to rooms one and two. Just as I arrived at the steps leading to the platform of the rooms, I saw a whole bunch of baby kraits at my feet. Luckily I was wearing trousers and trekking shoes and proceeded to kick them away with my foot. The guests had no idea what had happened. But after checking them in I went back and ordered a fullscale clean up job and a search for the mother. We found her in a rat borough just behind the room and chased her away. Left to Pradeep, the resident tribal maintenance manager, he would have gleefully killed each and every one of the reptiles for no fault of theirs. I had made it a rule that no snakes be killed on our property, a practice that I believe is born out of complete ignorance of their true habits and nature. The mother was over six feet long and by disturbing and frightening her enough I was convinced that she would not return. But we did take the precaution of collecting all the baby snakes and depositing them a kilometre away, for even the young krait has enough venom to kill a human.

The other problem snake that we have is the rat snake. Rooms seven to twelve were made of bamboo with a thatch roof. Birds and rats lived in abundance in the thatch and rat snakes moved in and cleaned them out. As long as the snakes were there we would have no rats or birds. Then due to the shortage of food the snakes would leave and the rats would return. This went on for years. The snakes did not disturb the guests as one could hardly ever see them. But one day, whilst chasing a rat on the bamboo beams a snake slipped and fell straight on the bed. Luckily the guest was not around and it was the housekeeping staff who got the shock of their lives. Rat snake bite can be painful. They are non-poisonous snakes but the pain of the bite and the shock of being bitten by a large snake that resembles a cobra can kill the weak of heart.

***

If ever there was a wild cobra that had come to like us and accept us in his domain, it was the dining hall cobra. I saw him for the first time whilst I was sitting in the raised dinning hall of the old units. It happened well before the large resort had been constructed in 1994, when we were still using the earlier facilities. There were no guests and I was alone. The staff were out on their usual chores. I was relaxing with a book on bridge. As is my usual practice, I put up my feet and settled down with a large cup of coffee.

I must have been reading for an hour when I saw a snake crawl up the bamboo pole facing the pool and slither onto the dining table. There it coiled itself comfortably and settled down with its expanded hood to study me in detail. It knew that I was there and even then it had decided to come out and settle itself on the table just a few feet from me. I kept on reading and the reptile kept up its vigil. This went on for another hour and it was when one of the staff came to clean the dining area that it slithered right past me into the stone wall below. Was I afraid? To tell the truth, when I first saw the cobra, I was. Then when it settled on the table, and subjected me to his unrelenting glare, I did feel uneasy. It was only when

Shaaz and Zoha in the crocodile and mahseer infested pool of the Cauvery river.

The wild boar that attacked Shaaz and Zoha, photographed the next day.

The right-chipped tusker minutes before he charged.

A perfect profile

Facing page: *Chocolate and Shampoo, two ponies who loved the forest as much as we did.*

Left: *The swimming pool at New Bush Betta.*

Right: *The pool overlooks the valley.*

Facing page:
Shot of a bedroom at Bush Betta.

The Mangala dam—a perennial water resource for the animals.

some time had passed and he made no move to attack, that I understood he meant me no harm, and was only on his regular day out. After that, I relaxed. The hour that I spent with him then became special. For some unknown reason, we trusted each other. He could have attacked me or I could have picked up a stick or a stone and killed him. But we managed a moment of trust that was so rare and so special between age-old rivals.

***

The clients who cause the biggest problems at Bush Betta are the ones who have no idea why they are in the bush. They hate going on safari, they refuse to step out of their rooms, and detest the outdoors. Naturally they find the place quite boring. The unfortunate part is that if anything has to go wrong, it will surely do so with them.

Once on a very cold and dark night we had an elderly couple check in quite late. They were given the best rooms that we had. The moment they arrived, we realized that they were problem clients. After dinner we took them to their rooms and having given them extra blankets and lanterns we did everything but tuck them into bed.

That night elephants raided the resort. I knew from the size of the raiders that it could only be Teresa and her herd. They went straight to the swimming pool and decided to quench their thirst. This herd was well known to us and it was not their first visit to our camp. The elephants knew that our property was safe grounds for them and were totally relaxed and having a whale of a time near the pool.

When the elderly couple heard the commotion, for their room was but a few feet from the pool, they lost their nerve and started screaming for help. The elephants were quite unperturbed by this noise and carried on having fun. Knowing that we could do nothing and most importantly should do nothing as long as the herd stood their ground, we called out and asked the couple not to come out of their rooms. Not knowing how they would react, I had climbed into the jeep, ready to go to their rescue if the need arose. Eventually, the old man could not take the commotion anymore and opened the door of his room to get away from the terrifying sounds that the pachyderms were making as they completed their bath. That is when I drove in with my lights out, bundled them both into the back seat and reversed to the stone cottage. Needless to say that night they checked out with the elephants and subsequently wrote a long letter to the travel agent complaining how we at Bush Betta had nearly caused their death!

I never did understand why people would want to come and view wildlife and then complain when the animals arrived at their doorstep.

***

One of the funniest incidents that I remember concerned rats. Right through 1991 to 1995, we had regular inbound guests coming in. Most were genuinely nice people who would enjoy the Bush Betta experience to the maximum. But in most large groups there would normally be a killjoy. The industry had got used to the tantrums thrown by these people and would warn us by sending out a 'KJC message', meaning 'Killjoy coming.' We would prepare ourselves adequately to deal with the situation.

It was on one such occasion that the Bangalore office received a KJC message from the travel agent. We decided to put her in the room immediately next to the manager. In case of any requirement he would rush in and address her problem before she disturbed the rest of the group.

As I have said before, there seems to be an unwritten law that whatever has to go wrong, does so with the killjoys. So it was with the lady. The first night went without any incident. But the problems started at breakfast.

The group was booked for an elephant safari. There were seven people in all, including the killjoy. Normally the departure time for the safari is nine in the morning, immediately after breakfast. We had twenty-eight eggs left over from the previous day and the supplies being bought fresh before each arrival, were not scheduled to come in that day. That morning each and every one of the twenty-eight eggs was consumed. Killjoy alone ate nine – and asked for more. She had a truly elephantine appetite!

Immediately after breakfast, all the other clients left to get ready for the trip but Killjoy stayed put waiting for more eggs to come. The service staff explained to her that this would take time, and that as it was getting late for the safari, maybe she could have the second round when she returned. She refused to budge and insisted that the eggs be bought. The manager sent the jeep to Mangala but it returned after fifteen minutes without the eggs, for there were none in the village. Killjoy still stood her ground. All the others left for the safari but she refused to move until she had had her fill of eggs. Finally the jeep had to be rushed to Gundulpet and returned with the precious eggs an hour and a half later.

Hot eggs were served at 11.30 a.m. Knowing that she would insist on an elephant safari after her breakfast we had requested that one of the pachyderms stand by. No sooner had she finished eating than she demanded to be taken on the ride. Expecting another confrontation and not getting one, she arrived back at lunch and was grumpy throughout the day.

All went well till the night. That was when the rats decided to pay her a visit. The lady had picked up an assortment of silk cocoons in Mandya and had these in a box under her bed. The next morning, all hell broke loose as Killjoy discovered the rats had eaten her silk cocoons. The manager was summoned, and he arrived to find her under the bed, photographing the remains of the cocoons. She even took detailed pictures of rat droppings next to the half-eaten bundles. By the time I arrived on the scene, she had worked herself up into a frenzy. I tried my best to calm her, and offered to replace the cocoons or pay her double the price she had paid for them. But she continued to rant for over an hour, threatening to sue us for the mental trauma that both she and the cocoons had suffered.

Finally, my patience ran out. The other guests were ready to depart, having loaded their luggage in the van. I asked Killjoy to give me the bill for the cocoons so that we could compensate her on the spot and settle the matter. That is when she crumbled. She had stolen the cocoons – and naturally had no bill or proof of purchase! When I told her that we would have to file a police complaint against her, she got into the van quietly and departed. We heard no more about the silk cocoons!

***

Another incident connected with the same room took place in 2001. The main resort was full and we had decided to stay in the old cottages. Sangeeta and I were in the adjoining room and Zoha was sleeping alone as Shaaz was with his friends at the main lodge. Zoha sleeps early and was in deep slumber well before we had returned. As she was used to the jungle she quite enjoyed sleeping alone. That night we slept without incident or so we thought. We were leaving for Bangalore the next day and I had instructed Swamy to load our luggage into the car. He came rushing back and said that a large cobra was skulking under Zoha's bed. On investigation we realized that the snake had crawled in through the open gap in the incomplete chimney early the previous evening. Zoha had slept with the snake next to her. I was positive it was the old cobra friend of mine from the dining hall.

Shampoo and Chocolate

Wilderness suits them.

– Guests at Bush Betta camp, 1995

Our children have grown up with animals – of both the wild and the house-trained variety. We had three dogs in our Bangalore house and another few in Bandipur. Then Zoha saw *Black Beauty*, the movie, and decided that it was time to get our own ponies.

I spoke to friends who owned stud farms and eventually, Marty Mahindra agreed to offload two teasers onto us. Soon after, Shampoo and Chocolate arrived at the farm in a tempo in 1996. As soon as they alighted from the tempo, they were led off to be shampooed and scrubbed with every conceivable perfumed soap that we could find in Gundulpet. It was during this inaugural bath that they were named by the kids. Zoha decided that the piebald, a blend of black and white, with a wonderful serene expression would be called Shampoo. Not to be outdone by his younger sister, Shaaz named Chocolate after the bar that he had in his hand. I doubt if it had anything to do with the colour even though she was a beautiful bay. Well-mannered and gentle, Shampoo was the perfect gentleman, the best kind of pony one could have for young children. Chocolate was an angel with them but for some inexplicable reason, a raging tyrant with the rest of us, biting, kicking and rolling her eyes at will. Only Shaaz and Zoha could approach her, and she allowed them complete liberty. They would crawl between her legs, pull her ears and her tail, only to be nuzzled in return.

We had built small stables for them and proceeded to spoil them rotten with love and affection. The ponies loved the stables but they loved their independence more. Within a few weeks of their arrival, they were out in the valley exploring their surroundings.

One day the Deputy Conservator of Forests asked me to accompany him into the park as he was also an avid wildlife photographer. Driving back on the Mangala dam road with the national park to the left and private forest to the right, we saw a herd of elephants. The light was perfect. It was the beautiful bright golden sun of the late afternoon that every photographer in the wild dies for. As the officer took out his zoom and focused the telephoto lens, his gaze fell on two ponies grazing happily with the elephants. I have never seen a government man get as angry as he did that day. He summoned the range officer and gave him the dressing down of his life for allowing ponies into the park.

The ranger was a friend of mine and knew full well that the ponies were mine. But he kept his counsel and merely assured his senior that he would take the most urgent and drastic action against the sod who had left his ponies to graze in the park. I too held my peace and chose not to inform the irate officer that the ponies were on private land and not in the national park. The elephants were in the wrong place.

One of our neighbours has a small resort. We are good friends even though we compete in the market. One night the ponies were found inside his reception. The neighbour being a horse lover himself, brought them back to Bush Betta, at around 3 a.m. He never complained.

We were not so lucky with some clients who were staying with us on a two-night package. They had heard a leopard sawing and elephants feeding next to their rooms on their first night, and had been too terrified to sleep. The next day they asked to be moved closer to the main reception. We did try and explain to them that there was no danger whatsoever from these animals as long as the guests stayed in their rooms but to no avail. We moved them into the suite closest to the new reception.

That night we were hit by a thunderstorm. Lightning roared and rumbled and the rain fell hard and heavy. It was around one in the morning when all the lights had been turned off that they heard a large animal approach their cottage. Then it had tried to push the door and break into the suite. Scared out of their wits, the guests double-locked the main door and bolted the inner one to their room.

The rustling and scraping on the doorway continued as long as the storm lasted. The guests had a torch but had no way of shining it on the animal from where they were. It was well after the cloudburst had passed and the rain had stopped that the sound ceased. The next morning we were met by a bleary-eyed couple who hadn't slept for over forty-eight hours. When we went to inspect their cottage to see if the night visitor had left behind any identifying traces, we realized it had been the ponies. The storm had driven them into the shelter of the veranda, and they had used the door to rub themselves! We offered the clients a free night's stay. They left.

***

It soon became a regular routine for Shampoo and Chocolate to break the poles of their stables and escape into the valley, and we would do a bi-weekly round up for them. Both Shaaz, then eight years old, and Zoha still a chubby little girl, just two years younger, insisted on going on the round ups. The ponies were usually to be found near the waterhole which lies adjacent to the main Mangala-Bandipur road about a half-kilometre from the farm.

The round up was actually quite a cumbersome exercise. Once outside the farm boundary, the ponies would not allow us to come close. If we tried to throw a noose around them, they would panic and run deep into the forest. Tracking them then was a full day's exercise. The trick lay in directing them towards the farm without alarming them and even if they were to panic, then to ensure that they ran towards the village, away from the forests, where they could be found with ease. At least seven of our staff had to be deployed for the round up. Five of them would stay behind the ponies forming a loose semi-circle, and walk towards them talking loudly to each other. The horses would start drifting just ahead of these people. Once they were close to the gate of the farm, the circle would tighten and the two who had stayed behind would plug any gap in the human dragnet if the ponies tried to break through.

On one of these round ups, Shaaz had insisted on standing near the gate with Zoha. There used to be a drainage trench running along the road and they were standing on its lip. The same Babu who had fainted at the sight of the bear, was chaperoning them.

As the dragnet neared the farm, instead of scaring the ponies, it startled a huge wild boar into a frenzied run. Babu was sure that it was the ponies approaching, and decided to intercept the animals just to the north of the gate in order to close the only exit route that they would have as they neared.

The children went with him. It was only as the animal broke cover that Babu saw that it was a boar and not the ponies. The boar having his only exit sealed off had two options, either to break the beat or charge through Babu and the kids. He chose the latter and broke into a run heading straight for the trio. On seeing the boar charging them, Babu panicked and deserting the kids, ran for the safety of the fence.

Shaaz, realizing he was alone, pushed his stunned sister into the ditch and dived in after her. The boar jumped the trench, his hooves grazing Zoha on the left shoulder as he cleared the ditch. With remarkable presence of mind for an eight-year-old, Shaaz had succeeded in removing them from the boar's direct line of attack. Had the boar hit the children, he would surely have killed them.

Babu, realizing that his actions may be construed as dereliction of duty, and having mastered the art of handling tricky situations, did what he did best – he fainted near the gate.

Meanwhile the children were trying to crawl out of the ditch only to find the ponies coming straight at them. Zoha was quite unafraid of her ponies and stood right in their path and waved them down. This shut their exit route and recognizing her, they trotted into the gate. Thanks to the thick sweaters and trousers the children were wearing, the adventure ended without any bones being broken by their dive into the ditch.

***

What was surprising was the way the ponies kept the big cats at bay. They showed complete disdain for the leopard that had for a while taken up residence in the camp. Our staff had actually seen them kicking the cat and driving it off the property. I have no idea how they handled the tigers but I am sure that on their numerous excursions into the jungles, they must have come across the big cat on more than one occasion.

Shampoo and Chocolate are now fourteen years old. They still break out and go into the forest but age has caught up with them, and they prefer to come back every evening. They are the best ponies one can find for riding in the forest for they know each and every smell of the jungle and even know how to handle the different threats. If one can get astride them, that is.

Zoha being an excellent rider manages to ride Shampoo but Chocolate will have no one on her back. She has produced over six foals. We lost only one to the leopard. The rest have been given to friends and two have been sent to the Embassy International Riding School in Bangalore.

The one that we lost was in August 2004. I was sitting with a few guests in the reception of the main lodge at night, when we heard the horses neighing. I was not too concerned, but Nanju who was with me, picked up a torch and ran out without saying a word. He came back shaking his head. He said that a leopard had descended on the foal and carried him into Suite 204, the furthermost room from the reception that was left unoccupied since its roof had sunk a few inches and as no one was staying in it, a big cat had decided to move in.

The pets and the people that we have had at Bandipur have stood apart for their unique characteristics. Whereas the animals got away by being animals, the humans had a tougher time of it, time living amongst the tribals.

The Human Jungle

In the city, it is the people who make the place.
In the jungles, it is the place that makes the people.

– Murli, tribal leader, when he came to Bangalore

If you even for the briefest of moments think that the problems that we had at Bush Betta were solely related to wildlife, you would be wrong. Apart from the animals in the jungles we had our own monsters, creatures that were human but were wilder than the wildest animals on earth. A book about our lives in the Mangala valley would not be complete if some of our encounters with these human animals were left unmentioned.

One of the more humorous incidents was one where I myself was the culprit. It was in 1992, the year that we began commercial operations at the small resort. A week before the Christmas-New Year season we had decided to clean out the swimming pool at the resort. I had picked up some diluted hydrochloric acid in a plastic can from Bangalore and was returning to the camp with it. I was travelling by bus as Sangeeta was already in Mangala with the children. I had taken a seat in front just next to the exit. When the bus reached the Chamrajpet turn off (the main approach to Mysore road was closed for some reason) in Bangalore city, it took a sharp turn to the right. The can fell to the side and the cap flew open. The metal floor of the bus started to fume mildly as the acid ate into the plate. People started shouting that there was a bomb on the bus and some screamed that the bus was on fire. Panic broke out in the vehicle as passengers tried to jump out of the small windows and even some buxom women clad in saris, threw themselves at the openings trying to squeeze their way out before the bus blew up.

Luckily it had been raining and there were puddles of water alongside the road. I told the driver to stop the bus and hefting the leaking can, threw it out of the door. Then I ran down and splashed some water on the eroding metal. The burning stopped but the panic persisted. The bus conductor gave me a resounding slap, loud enough for everyone on the bus to hear and then whispered to me to jump off the bus and run but not before he had divested me of a thousand rupees. Leaving my bag with my clothes behind, I ran into the side streets. Just before I turned the corner I looked back for one last time and was flabbergasted at the sight that met my eyes. Seven fat female bottoms stuck out of the windows, with people pulling them from both sides. Men on the road were trying to pull them out while the passengers within were jerking them back into the bus. About a few hundred yards down, I caught an auto and disappeared as fast as I could. This was definitely an occasion when retreat was the better part of valour!

***

Being miles away from urban life meant that the resort's permanent residents had two perpetual requirements. Drink and sex. Getting hold of a bottle was not so difficult as

Mangala has its own illicit liquor den that could supply most forms of drink. The libido was not so easy to deal with – and to make things worse, the fresh air of the valley and the many hours with nothing much to do, seemed to have a Viagra-like effect!

Those who were married, or the good-looking youngsters who often scored a hit with members of the inbound groups, did not do too badly. The problem lay with the not so good-looking ones, who would have to take the bus to Mysore to score on a free day, and the elderly.

One such manager was an elderly person who I thought was a really nice human being. But as it turned out, I was wrong.

We used to get a lot of foreign guests who were touring South India and would stop over for a couple of days at the camp. One afternoon, I had taken a group to the safari and was gone for over three hours. One of the guests had decided to stay behind, as she wanted to relax with a book and many cups of tea.

On my return from the safari one of our contractors, Nagraj who could just about manage to speak English, had this to say to me, and insisted on saying it in his own way.

'Saar, I standing alone under platform of dining haal, (which is an eight-foot high wooden projection) I changing burnt wiring that has disturbing us for one week. People of dining haal not able seeing me and as I going about my working in silent, nobody above knowing I am being there.'

Nagraj carried on in this vein until he had told me the whole story. It transpired that the manager, whom I had thought was such a saintly and respectable old man, had taken it upon himself to explain to the lady the mating rituals of various animals in the forest – with supporting actions. It was when he came to the human of the species, that Nagraj decided that enough was enough, and jumped out from under the ledge. The lady, who had by then turned the colour of the setting sun, was emboldened by his presence to give the offending manager a resounding slap across his face. The trusty Nagraj then caught him by the shirt and led him off to the stone cottage, where he had locked him in the main room to await my arrival.

I returned from the safari to be confronted by an angry woman threatening us all that if the fiend of a manager was not thrown out of the premises she would take the bus to the police station and report him. I complied with alacrity, and the manager left, never to be seen again.

***

After this disaster, I thought it best to hire a married couple to look after the resort. Having searched in vain for a long time, I finally chanced upon a very pleasant and hard-working duo, and took them on.

I was so relieved that at last I had responsible people to take care of Bush Betta that slowly over a period of a year, I handed over the accounting reins to them. The husband was great with people and a perfect host for the resort. He even managed the cashbook and started saving on the purchases. She took care of the kitchen, maintenance and housekeeping. That year we had a great season with me being able to spend more time with my family in Bangalore and the resort showing great improvement with clients coming back really happy even without me being there. I gave the couple a raise and a bonus.

December is peak season for us. It was the first week of December in 1998 when we had, after a long time, a packed house at Bush Betta. And it was also for the first time that I could relax at home in Bangalore content in the knowledge that Bush Betta was well taken care of and there would be no problems with the clients.

Little did I know the drama that was to unfold at the resort.

I was playing bridge at our Bangalore house when I got an urgent call to rush to Bandipur. I was given no reasons but just asked to get there as soon as possible. I called Narendar, our director based in Mysore and was told that even he had gone to the resort. His wife had no idea what was happening but knew that something was seriously wrong.

Rush I did and got to the resort late in the morning. I arrived to find the guests relaxed and checking out. They were very happy with their stay and complimented me on the great time that they had had with our team. After the last guest had gone I called a staff meeting to find out what the problem was. The story that they narrated was one for the films.

Our cook, Sharad, as was his wont, took the onus on himself to explain to me the frightening events of the previous night.

The collections for that day had exceeded Rs 80,000. The guests had gone to bed early as they had been out in the bush the whole day and were tired. The manager and his wife had thrown a party for the staff and brought in a few cases of liquor from the local shop. Most of our staff had drunk more than they could stand and were soon in deep slumber, spread thin all over the resort. It was only Sharad and Nanju who sensed that something was amiss, and remained alert. They would take the bottle that was offered to them and then pour it out when the manager and his wife were not looking.

So they were stone cold sober when, around midnight, a taxi drove into the camp. They asked the driver what he was doing there, as the guests were not checking out till morning.

He told them that he had been asked to report to Bush Betta at night to carry two people to Bangalore airport in time for the first Mumbai flight. He was also carrying two air tickets to Mumbai. All had been paid for by cash.

Nanju and Sharad acted drunk till they saw the manager head for the office and open the cash box. This was when Sharad sprang out of hiding and apprehended him redhanded. The manager was shocked to see Sharad and Nanju and asked them what the problem was and why they were not drinking and enjoying the party with all the rest.

Sharad confronted the manager and accused him of being a thief. He said that now they would use the same taxi to take the couple to the Gundulpet police station. The manager pushed the cook out of his way and ran to the cab only to find the driver missing. Meanwhile both Nanju and Sharad closed in from both sides to apprehend him. The manager had jumped into the cab and was trying to negotiate a quick getaway by offering them a part of the booty. Sharad kicked the door and said he would break the window with a rock if he didn't unlock it. Nanju meanwhile had picked up a wheel spanner and was looking around for the wife. What he saw made his blood run cold. She was stalking the cook with a butcher's knife that she had picked up from the kitchen. Just as she was about to strike at Sharad, Nanju screamed out a warning. Sharad spun around to see the woman lunging at him. The cook is a very tall man. He towered above the woman and before she could reach him, he had hit her hard on the head. She screamed out in pain and fell over backwards with the momentum of the hit. The manager saw his wife falling and rushed out.

Meanwhile Nanju who still had the wheel spanner, sprinted around the vehicle and hit him hard on the shoulder with the tool. They divested the couple of other hidden weapons and shut them in the stone cottage, intending to keep them there, far from the guests, until I arrived. The taxi driver, in the meantime, seeing the ruckus, had fled into the night.

Unfortunately, the crooked couple managed to break the window of the bathroom and escape on the early morning bus. I could not be contacted as I had already left Bangalore.

I arrived to find the money intact and the staff reeling under a severe hangover. The innocent tribals had not suspected anything. It was only the cook and Nanju who had known that something was not right and had waited for the manager and his wife to make their move.

It was too late to report the matter to the police as the culprits had already fled the scene of the crime. In any case the money was secure and we decided against filing an official complaint. We just handed over a letter to the police indicating that nothing was missing but that maybe an alert should be sounded for two smooth operators who had the entire heist planned well in advance.

***

One incident nearly had me booted out of my house. It took place in the dry month of March in 1994. One day when I was sitting in our office at Bangalore, in walked two gorgeous girls who said they would like to stay with us for a week. Proficient businessman that I am, I saw quick dollars coming our way. Two foreign clients staying for a week was good money. But when I told them what the charges would be, they decided that it was beyond their budget. Then one of them started crying and said that she so desperately wanted to live in the Indian bush and would be heartbroken if she had to go back home without doing so. I melted with ease and offered them a deal. I said that if they would work at the resort for a month then they could stay free of cost. They jumped at the offer and left for Bandipur the same day.

We were soon to follow as Vivek Paul, the head of a multinational company and a dear friend of ours, was visiting us with his family. My wife was none too pleased when she learnt that I had hired two young and pretty foreign lasses, and decided she needed to check things out at the resort.

We arrived at Bush Betta over a long weekend expecting to find everything running smoothly in the hands of the two managers. What followed was complete disaster. The girls had taken over the two best suites that we had blocked for Vivek and his family, and had hung all their washing outside to dry. We drove in to find them sun bathing near the pool with their bras and underwear hanging on the windows. Seeing that Sangeeta was fuming, my loyal staff quietly disappeared from view.

Sharad was sent for and questioned. When Sharad explained that the girls were not acting as managers but as demanding guests, a fit was thrown and I was sent for. Knowing that times were bad I had slipped out and hid in Gundulpet for the day on the pretext that I had meetings with the Tehsildar. Sangeeta had to take her anger out on someone. She sent for Vivek and said that it was his duty as my best friend to collect the money for the days that the two girls had stayed at Bush Betta. The poor man was an excellent negotiator but had to use the utmost charm to convince the girls that the management had had a change of heart and they were now required to pay for their stay. The meeting lasted two hours. At the end of it, a beaming Vivek handed over the entire money that was due to Sangeeta. The girls were shoved into the CEO's car and despatched via the first bus available to Kerala. I have no idea where they went for they never did write to me. I have always wondered why.

That night I came in late and slept in the room adjacent to my friend's. The next day, having allowed enough time for my wife to cool down, I met everyone at breakfast and behaved as though I knew nothing about the girls' departure. I managed to put up a great performance and acted really surprised to find them missing.

It was only when we returned to Bangalore that I refunded my friend the money that he had paid out of his own pocket to Sangeeta, telling her that he had got it off the girls!

Then there was the time when one of our guests burnt the bathroom down. Nandan and Rohini Nilekani had kept a lit candle on the plastic flush tank at night. Even as they slept the whole toilet went up in flames. After that event, we would send out the night staff to put out the candles in every bathroom. When I next met Nandan he was driving on M.G. Road in Bangalore. He shouted across the divider asking me to buy shares in his company. He offered me Infosys shares at Rs 10 per share. I laughed and waved him away. How dumb can a man get? Had I had picked up a few hundred shares, I would have been a multimillionaire by now.

Mr B: An Expert in the Family

In elephant jungle
When he say right – you turn left
When he say left – you turn right
When he say safe – You run for your life.

– Nanjundiah, July 1991, on Mr B

Before I met the tribals of Mangala, there were a few people who were instrumental in introducing me to the wilderness.

For my wife and I, my cousin Bakhtiyar Ansari was our greatest ally during all earlier sojourns into the jungle.The son of a tea planter, he had spent his youth in the elephant-infested jungles of the Annamalai in Tamil Nadu. We were naïve enough to assume that he knew the bush and both Sangeeta and I put immense faith in the numerous decrees that he would pass whenever we were out in the bush. Even whilst at Hyderabad we would be out exploring the nearby jungles almost every week, usually in his company. Out of respect for his knowledge, we addressed him as Mr B.

On one wild holiday with my uncle Nawab Nazeer Yar Jung, after breakfast at Jungle Hut in Masinagudi, which is about forty kilometres or an hour and a half's drive from Mangala, Mr B suggested that we go for a drive. We set off in our little green Maruti Suzuki along the Moyar canal road. There is a crossroad at Masinagudi, the road west heading towards the Singara powerhouse, and the one east leading to the Moyar village. The Moyar canal runs all along this track, to the south and parallel to the tar road. In the drier months, it is an excellent route for sighting elephants.

Mr B declared that there would be no elephants on the left of the road. He said that we would only see the animals to the right. Mr B was driving and we must have gone a few kilometres when we saw a herd of elephants just across the channel and as decreed by the expert, to our right. Stopping the car, my uncle, Mr B and I walked the short distance to the canal to get a better view of the animals.

Sangeeta, who had never been into the forests till then, said she would stay in the car. Mr B and I were busy soaking in the fantastic sight before us, when we heard the Maruti start up and revv its engine. Knowing that something was wrong and fearing that someone maybe harassing her we rushed back. What we found was my wife at the wheel and the engine running. All the windows were up. We looked around and saw nothing.

'Bhabhi, what happened?' asked Mr B.

'The moment you went into the jungle, two elephants came out of the opposite bush just ten yards away, and headed towards the canal. Since you had told us no elephants could come from the left, I was taken by surprise,' she told us.

She went on, 'I was terrified of the elephants and had put up the windows when I realized you were in danger as well. So I started the car and revved the engine in order to warn you.'

Instead of being grateful to Sangeeta for having saved our

lives, Mr B burst out laughing. 'How can you be frightened of elephants,' he asked us between chuckles. 'I would never turn around or run from them, I know how to control these cowardly beasts.'

Our experiences with Mr B started in 1986 but it was on Shaaz's first birthday on the 28th of January 1989 that we actually realized his capabilities in the bush. We had come to Bandipur camp to celebrate the birthday but, having tasted the comforts of Jungle Hut, we decided to keep a room at Bandipur but stay the night in Masinagudi. Immediately after dinner, having cut the birthday cake, we took off to meet Joe Mathais, the owner of Jungle Hut.

It is about eight kilometres from Bandipur to the Kakkanhalla border. Just after the Bandipur camp there are a few waterholes quite close to the main road. One can normally see elephants in this area. At night the pachyderms prefer to feed on the fresh grass that sprouts in profusion next to the road.

'There will be no elephants to the right of the road,' Mr B had proclaimed before leaving camp. By then we were a little wiser in his ways, and promptly looked only to the right. Sure enough, it was on our right, at the spot where the safari track turns into Kullukmallekatte, that we passed a herd of elephants standing a mere thirty yards off the road, majestic in the translucent moonlight.

We had come all the way from Bangalore to see the mighty beasts and there they were, standing just a few yards from us. Wanting to spend time with them we decided to turn back. I suggested to my cousin that maybe we should go another hundred yards before turning the car around. He would have none of that. 'Leave it to me!' was all we heard as he braked and reversed hard left to flash the beam of the headlights on the group.

The small Maruti has very strong reverse lights. In this harsh glare I saw a large elephant standing right behind us and in our direct path. I yelled at Mr B to stop but as usual, he overruled me, calling me a weakling who had lost his nerve in the darkness of the night.

I closed my eyes as the little car drove into the rump of the animal with a shallow thump. We were thrown back as Mr B jammed on the brakes. The poor elephant let out a scream of terror even as Mr B bellowed equally loudly, changed gears and threw the car in front. I just about got a glimpse of the elephant disappearing into the thick bush as we sped on.

From Kakkanhalla, the Theppakadu forest office in the Madhumalai Sanctuary and National Park is another seven kilometres. Mr B was driving at breakneck speed, oblivious to our pleas to slow down. As the road descends and enters the camp, there is a blind left turn. We took this curve at well over fifty kilometres an hour and as we completed the turn, the beam of the headlights settled on something lying across the road.

Both Sangeeta and I yelled for Mr B to stop. Mr B wears what we in India call soda glasses which are thick and heavy. Without them Mr B is blind. Unfortunately even with them Mr B is blind.

Mr B retorted, 'Bah! You city dwellers are chicken, it's nothing but a log.' And insisting that it was only deadwood, he bashed on regardless. We must have been fifteen yards from 'the log' when it rose up from the road like a ghost and stood glaring at us.

Mr B screamed, 'Leopard' and jammed down hard on the brake. Poor Shaaz flew from the back and somehow managed to land on my lap as the car came to a skidding halt. The animal stood his ground. He was huge. Being a cold winter night he had settled down on the tar, which retains heat through the night.

We spent ten minutes with the cat as he moved from the road to the lantana thicket in which he settled and continued to stare fixedly at us with his head on his paws. He was probably wishing we would leave so that he could get back to the warmth of the road.

Leaving the animal behind and ecstatic that we had seen both the elephants and a huge leopard in such a short time, we drove on.

At Theppakadu, there is a fork in the road, with the right going to Ooty via Gudalur and the left towards Masinagudi and the short route to Ooty. Ooty from this camp was seventy-two kilometres via the former and only thirty-six on the latter.

The road to Gudalur is along the Theppakadu river and assures one of elephant sightings in summer. But the Masinagudi road is much better for game sighting.

Immediately after the Theppakadu bridge to the right is the elephant camp. A few kilometres past this camp is the safari track ascending right and up the hill. This is the Mandradia VIP road that has excellent game viewing. Soon after this turnoff, lying next to the road again to the right, is an outcrop of rock and in these rocks is a perennial waterhole. I have seen most animals of the area at this pool.

The road passes through thick bush soon after this waterhole. The banks on the sides are quite high and standing on the right escarpment, silhouetted against the full moon, was a huge bull elephant. No sooner had we come abreast of him than we realized that the road ahead was completely blocked by a mass of huge lumbering bodies. The whole herd was using the highway. Either the matriarch signalled the tusker or he took it upon himself to rid his breeding herd of the newly arrived menace. He charged.

Mr B was in the direct path of impact. Screaming, 'Chaarge', he threw the car into reverse. The elephant moved down the hill with incredible agility and was soon thundering down the centre of the road after us as we reversed. He must have pursued us for a few hundred yards but to us it seemed an eternity. Finally as we neared the waterhole I saw him back off. We drove on in reverse. The turn off to Mandradia flashed past and we were still reversing, the elephant camp arrived and we were still reversing. Where I had been frightened seeing the elephant thundering down on us now I was petrified at the thought of us missing the turn to the Theppakadu bridge and crashing down into the cold waters of the river fifty feet below. Our pleas fell on deaf ears as we drove on at terrifying speeds – backwards.

How Mr B managed to stay on the road is anyone's guess. But stay on he did and kept up the incredible pace till we had reached the bridge. There, under the street lamp he turned the car around and without saying a word started to head back for Bandipur. All plans to proceed to Jungle Hut were forgotten. Not one of us spoke on the drive back for the last thing that we needed was to attract the wrath of the expert by breaking the silence. It was two in the morning when we reached our room at the camp and crawled into the safety of our beds. So much for never running from elephants! But at least Shaaz had had an unforgettable first birthday, thanks to Mr B.

***

I must accept that one of the prettiest drives I have been on was with Mr B when he took us to the Western Catchment. One of the wardens of the Madhumalai sanctuary was a close family friend. Mr Palniappan or Uncle Palni to us was a wonderful human being. He was loved by all and had not a single bad bone in him. But the one thing that Mr B could not stand about Uncle Palni was the way he drove his jeep. Like most planters he drove fast and hard and treated the vehicle without any emotion. Mr B hated sitting in the car when anybody else but he was driving, and he simply abhorred poor Uncle Palni's driving. Nonetheless Uncle Palni was the warden and it was his jeep and there was no way that Mr B was going to get to drive on the route to the beautiful catchments of the Niligiris.

Uncle Palni loved sambar. Whenever he saw one he would rumble 'Sambharrr' with great pleasure and brake to a jerking halt to spend as much time observing the deer as the animal allowed.

We had left with a packed lunch at eight in the morning. We drove hard and we drove fast. We drove into every deep rut that the road possessed. The jeep was taking a hell of a beating and the more we drove the sulkier Mr B became. Finally he could take it no more. Pretending that he had seen an animal on the hill, he made us stop. Then he decided to walk as we had our tea.

The countryside was simply incredible. Just after Pykara there is a dirt track that proceeds in a westerly direction. Pykara itself is at 7,000 feet above sea level and the route westwards does not climb much higher but clings to the hillside in a precarious manner as it meanders along.

The hills are quite bare with superb grazing. Shola forests can be seen snaking all the way up. Sambar are found in abundance and there was a moment when we thought we had seen a tiger emerge from the shola, way up on the hill. It must have been something for the sambar broke into their usual chorus of alarm calls on spotting danger. Even the Toda buffaloes looked in the direction of the hills with their ears up but after a few moments when they had grouped into five solid bulls, they relaxed. They knew that not even the largest of tigers would dare to attack when they were thus united.

The most beautiful parts of the valley are the exquisite blue lakes that can be seen every few kilometres. It is like looking down into a translucent mirror. The perennial water is spring-fed and once upon a time used to hold millions of trout but ever since the introduction of carp, the trout have dwindled and now you would have to be really lucky if you were to catch one in these waters.

There used to be a time when these hills held thousands of *Hemitragus hylocrius*. Commonly known as the Nilgiri tahr, these beautiful wild mountain goats would flit on the mountains in great numbers. Leave alone the animals, nowadays even their droppings cannot be found.

But from the thriving prey species in the area it would be safe to deduce that tiger numbers would be on the rise in these forests. The area is so inaccessible and so full of game that it is perfect for the shy cats. The tiger unlike the leopard has never got used to the presence of humans. Rightfully so for whenever he does come in contact with the human race it is the tiger that suffers.

Descending at top speed towards a blue lagoon, on a terribly rutted road, we heard a familiar sound. It was a 'snap bang' and then the jeep lurched to the left as the leaf spring broke. Mr B, who had by now worked himself into a rage, refused to even look under the vehicle to see what had happened. It was after much pleading and begging by Sangeeta that he was persuaded to sacrifice his own belt to the spring. Later he told me that he would have sleepless nights, reminiscing about that drive and the way old Uncle Palni handled the jeep. Sadly, Uncle Palni died of a heart attack some years ago, and we lost a dear friend whose house was always open to us at any time of the day or night.

Apart from the trip that Kishore Mallya and I had done in 1985, I owe my being in Bandipur today entirely to Mr B for it was he who first introduced Sangeeta and I to the elephant forests of South India. His wife – who also happens to be my cousin – is in my view one of the best assets that a man could want in the jungles. She can cook up a superb bush meal in seconds and has done so many a time when Sharad our cook has disappeared with Nanju for their secret rendezvous at the local bar. She understands and respects wildlife like very few that I know. Our misadventures with him notwithstanding, the entire Jung family at Bandipur, tribals included, look forward to Mr and Mrs B's visits – though presently, Mr B's preoocupation with looking after one of the properties of the Nizam of Hyderad does not allow him much time.

Narrations of a Tribal Smuggler

There is no greater controversy in wildlife conservation than the numbers game. Scientists, politicians, bureaucrats and the public, all play the game with great enthusiasm.

– Vivek Menon, Director, Wildlife Trust of India

Once we had bought the land in Mangala, the urge to explore the valley took over. My guide on most of these adventures was Nanjundiah, the tribal who soon became my most trusted friend in the forest. I have travelled the bush with many an expert but in the elephant jungles of India there is nobody that I would rather have beside me than Nanju.

Born in 1960 on a wet and windy December morning to Madhevamma, whilst his father Jonia was out tilling the land to bring back their ration for the day, he lived a life free from most needs till he got married. He was one of the five males born to the family. He grew up roaming the jungles with the cattle of the village and when he was strong enough to man the till, started helping in the fields. On seeing an elephant herd he would follow it till evening when he would bring back the cattle. He would creep up to a bull elephant and spend hours observing him without the animal ever knowing of his presence. He had fine-tuned the expertise of tracking deer and he would be in the middle of a herd before they realized that they had a human in their midst. Gaur would at times descend the Burrenkatte valley and he would be waiting. He boasted of hiding in thick bush and caressing them as they walked past. Having spent many hours with him in the bush, I do believe he has the ability to do so. It was with him that I first touched a wild elephant from a vehicle.

When I started eco development in Mangala valley, Nanju was the first person to join me and has stayed ever since. He helped me in my quest for the elusive working formula of eco-tourism as a tool for conservation as well as a source of revenue for all concerned. His experience in the bush has helped us perfect the wild experience in the Indian jungle.

At the time of writing this book he is fighting all odds to establish Bush Betta as the leader in eco-tourism in India. His son Ishkantiah manages his lands while his daughter Rainuma is studying. His house has a telephone from which most calls in the village are made, and he is looked up to by all who know him as a source of wisdom and knowledge. The villagers seek his advice on all manner of problems, and I have learnt to respect his counsel on most matters to do with the bush.

Of the many nights that I spent with Nanjundiah in the jungles, one just begs to be told. It was in November 1992, during a lull in the tourist season, soon after the cold winds of the monsoons had washed the jungle clean that we had decided to pitch camp barely four kilometres from home, next to a natural waterhole. Nanju said that the best place to view game in these months of plentiful feed was here on the eastern edge of the Mangala valley. We were there mainly to observe the trend of the migrating elephant herds.

On the first night itself we saw tiger, gaur, leopard and elephant not to mention the line of deer that would file past at regular intervals. We had decided to halt at this serene oasis for five nights and were inundated with elephants but none that were migrating. They seemed to be using this patch of small shrub as a platform for their daily raids into the adjoining fields.

Early on the third morning just as dawn was setting in, we heard the sound of approaching humans. I was immediately on my guard but noting Nanju's calmness I relaxed. Nanju never panics and therein lies his strength. He knew instinctively that they were smugglers and had rightly decided that an aggressive stance would be a safer option. There were five of them and in the diffused light of the morning it appeared to me that they were carrying something on their heads and immediately on seeing us, had thrown their load into the bush.

Seeing Nanju and me, four of them disappeared into the thicket and only the leader proceeded to come into our camp. He knew we were not from the department but was playing it safe by approaching us alone. Nanju and the poacher got into a hushed discussion. Not knowing what was going on, I chose to remain ignorant.

The leader told Nanju that they had just come up the Moyar ditch and would under normal circumstances camp at the waterhole till sunset when they would proceed to Jakkalli. I was surprised to see the leader greet Nanju with such respect and reverence. I knew that our man was a popular tribal leader in Mangala but had no idea of the reach of his fan club.

Till date I do not know who they were and I never did bother to find out their names for I really did not want to get into anything illegal if that is what it was.

Out of respect for one in the bush, according to jungle tradition, Nanju invited the group in for tea. All five filed into camp looking warily about them, but relaxed once they realized that we were no threat. The others in the group hardly spoke and remained aloof for most of the time, but the leader seemed inclined to talk. He said that he had been waiting to meet me for quite some time as he had heard talk within the tribal community about the work that Nanju and I were doing for them.

He asked us if they could stay with us till nightfall. Since they were not on our land, we were hardly in a position to refuse. Having settled that he was with us for the day, the leader said that he would like to tell me a story. He added that what he was going to say was the truth and it was up to me to believe it or not. He appeared to be something of a poet, and when he spoke, it was with much theatrical embellishment. I had no problems with that as I had all the time in the world, and was always ready for a good yarn. But before beginning the story he made it clear that he was changing the name of the person in order to protect him from the law.

Nanju served us all a round of tea. Having slurped the residue off the saucer, the man took a reefer out of his pouch and lit it with great care. He offered me the first drag but I told him that I did not smoke. Sitting on my bamboo mat, he took a deep drag and, after having taken Nanju's permission to proceed, began his story. This is what he told us.

***

The cloudburst was unduly harsh and it was as if the gods were sending a message to earth. Lightning flashed over the dripping hills and resonated in the mountains. The small streams had become raging torrents of water carrying with them the last written tales of the wilderness. All signs in the bush, the spoor of animals, the dung heaps, the drag marks and the different smells had disappeared as the ground took on a virgin look.

On this fresh earth, our storyteller told us, was born a healthy, chubby, round-faced boy. He was born to a vivacious young tribal woman. The father of the child was away when she had felt the first pangs of childbirth. She was alone in the hut and where she would have normally gone out into the bush to deliver, as is the tradition with her people, this time the storm prevented her from stepping out and she delivered the child in a corner of her thatched lean-to.

She did not even have to slap the ward for the sound of thunder rolled into the tiny hut and the child started to cry. He gasped in huge loads of smoke-filled air and after a few minutes, settled down to the lilting sound of rain. She cut the umbilical cord with a new blade that she had preserved for a month.

Her husband returned early next morning to the good news that he was a father. He held the child high in the air and pointing him into the rising sun named him Bhama.

Bhama grew up in the jungles around Jakalli. He did try his best to attend school but his mind was lost to the deep forest. That he passed every exam that he sat for even though his attendance was less than five percent amazed everyone.

With each passing year, his knowledge of the jungles and its animals grew manifold for he would walk alone into the bush every morning and come back in time for the evening meal. His father believed that the boy should be allowed to do as he liked and did not interfere in his life. On the contrary, whenever he had the time he would accompany him into the bush, only to observe what the youngster would do the entire day in the forests.

What he saw, he approved. The young boy would pick up the spoor of an animal and follow it till he had deciphered its every movement. He would observe what the animals ate and his mind registered their every need. He would make it a point to join up with the other tribals in the jungle and learn the medicinal values of the herbs and plants that grew in profusion. His education was in the forest, about the jungle.

At this point I interrupted and asked the storyteller if he was referring to our Nanju. Giving me no answer, he continued his narration as though I had not spoken.

Young Bhama saw his father work the fields and noticed that he disappeared every week for a day or two. He would vanish into the night and come back the next morning with bundles of money in his pocket. The boy would always wonder where he went and longed to accompany him on these sojourns. It was only when he completed his twelfth year that his father, whilst tilling the field, handed him a sickle and said that that night he would take little Bhama with him.

The boy was greatly excited. Running home he told his mother the plan. Instead of rejoicing with him, she broke into sobs and tears ran down her cheeks, whether of joy or pain he could not tell. If they were shed in anguish then he would need to find out the reason. He wanted to get back from his maiden journey and then confront her.

His mother prepared a parcel of ragi roti (dry thick pancake) and green chilly chutney. He had made a small bundle with his blanket and sickle and sat ready for his father's return. Early that evening, his father's best friend fetched him and explained to his mother that the others were waiting at the drop off.

They headed south and hiked up the Burrenkatte track, past Mangala village and by the time they skirted Colony village it was dark. The use of torches was banned but each person was carrying one. This was purely for an emergency.

They trekked in the dark crossing the elephant trench and entered the national park just south of Colony.

They heard elephants further south and turning east into a shallow valley, headed towards the Kathenburra stream. The stream was flowing and most wild animals east of Rolling Rock Falls on the Moyar-Kathenburra track would descend down to this water at around this time. They spooked a herd of sambar, which went thundering westwards towards the elephants and then skirted a lone tusker that they heard splashing in the river.

They followed a track heading east from the stream and after fifteen minutes of hard walking came upon a band of men sitting silently, sipping tea. Bhama recognized his father and bowed in respect. He was dying of excitement but there was no way that he would allow any of these seasoned forest goers to sense his true feeling. That would be viewed as a sign of immaturity. He kept grim and straight-faced even though his hands shook as he hugged his elders in respectful embrace.

Each and every man recognized the fact that it was Bhama's day of blooding. Today he would be inducted into their society as an equal.

As he stood amongst the small group of six squatting adults, his father spent a few minutes explaining to him their plan for the night and the emergency routines in case of animal attack.

Bhama learnt that day that in case of an elephant charge or snakebite it was the first man that would get hit and in case of a tiger it would be the last person in the group trekking in a single file, who would get picked up. A sloth bear would blunder straight through the line and could hit anyone in the file.

His father had gone on to explain that if an elephant

charged, the leader would make the call on what had to be done. It was his decision whether to run or stand and call its bluff. If he ordered them to run then it would be every man for himself. Else they would have to withstand the charge. If the problem was with one of the larger cats it was mandatory for the group to stay close together and stand their ground and having stopped the first charge of the animal, slowly move away from the danger.

Here I interrupted the flow of words once again and, looking at Nanju, asked him if it was indeed he who was the boy in the story. Nanju shook his head vehemently and said he had no idea who the man was talking about. I could tell that our storyteller was unaccustomed to interruptions and each time that I butted in he would grimace in annoyance. Without waiting for me to finish speaking, he carried on.

After Bhama's lesson was complete, they started to move again. The group had been waiting for the boy at the drop off into the Moyar gorge. They descended straight down into the void. As the youngster was not allowed to use his torch, the only thing he could see was inky darkness and empty space. They would have to find their way down into the gorge on touch and instinct alone. Bhama had never been into the canyon but had heard numerous stories of people who had done this route before. Some had died, killed by elephant, sloth bear and tiger. A few had simply slipped and fallen over the ledge into the river below.

The path that the men were taking had been cut by elephants and was exceedingly steep and dangerous. Elephants have a knack of moving on difficult terrain and actually find it easier to move on these tracks than do humans. For the small group of men it had been slow going. The men travelled single file, with Bhama's uncle, his father's brother, leading the group. Bhama had a rough rope tied around his waist with which he was connected to his father. It took them an hour to get to the river. There they rested with the Moyar powerhouse only a few hundred yards to the east of them. The brilliance of its yellow lights had been visible to them all along their descent.

Then they headed north and walked fast as the path was well-trodden and used by man and animal alike. Just before Rolling Rock Falls, they cut south and headed up another steep path into Madhumalai.

Bhama knew that climbing was easier than descending. They crested the lip of the gorge within half an hour and sped onwards for another fifteen minutes. Hidden from all sides in a depression lay their treasure. Cut pieces of teak and rosewood. The smell of sandalwood was hanging in the air but it was from old shavings scattered around. His father explained that they did not do sandal, as it was very dangerous. They confined themselves to the other valuable timber. Bhama did wonder how smuggling for sandalwood could be more dangerous than carrying other wood. Both were illegal and carried the same risks. It was only later that he understood the true meaning of what his father had said.

As it was still dark, they built a small fire and sat around it planning their next move. Each one opened his little parcel of food. The meal was so sparse and dry that it was consumed within minutes. After resting for half an hour, Bhama's father gave the signal to move out.

They doused the fire with mud and lined up for their loads. Each one hefted a seven-foot long log around two to three feet in diameter. Balancing it on their heads, they departed back the way they had come. The youngster was given a thinner pole to carry. This he picked up with immense pride. It made him feel that now he was an adult, part of the inner core of his father's team.

They headed down back into the abyss and it took them well over an hour to get down. As they waded across the stream, little Bhama thought he heard a heavy animal moving in front. He stood still as he was the third from the front just behind his father. His father stopped with him and strained his neck forward to put meaning to the sound that they had just heard.

The leader, sensing that the line had stopped, quickly and silently stepped off the track and froze. That is when the elephant charged.

The big tusker had been recovering form a painful injury to his hind leg. He knew that he had been shot and was angry with himself for having left the confines of the gorge. He had moved well east of the Anaikatti. He had been travelling with speed and had not even stopped to rest as he crossed the dangerous forests on his way into the Biligiriranganabetta. That was when he heard a shot and felt his rear leg go numb. It had been difficult to move but he had run, hobbling on three legs and dragging his injured foot behind, for he knew that if he stayed in the area he would be killed.

He had entered the gorge well below the power-generating unit, as the descent there was shallower and less steep. He had limped along the river and had decided to ascend the gorge by the same track that had been used by the smuggling party.

He had been resting when he smelt the familiar odour of man and froze, suspecting that the hunters had followed him into the gorge. He slipped into the thick bush to the side of the track and waited. The unsuspecting group walked straight into him.

The leader had no idea what hit him. The elephant had only been ten yards from him before he had launched his attack. Seething in pain and anger the elephant smashed his trunk into the crouching man and then looming over the half-broken body drove a heavy tusk into the midriff.

Bhama had felt the ground tremble as the brute descended upon them and then he heard the snapping of bone followed by the slush sound of the wind being driven out of the poor victim. He had heard his uncle say, 'Run, Maga, run.' (Maga is the Kannada word for son.) Then he heard a muted scream as his uncle was impaled on the tusk. Bhama knew that his uncle was dead. His father ordered him to throw his load and run. Soon in the blackness of night it was every man for himself.

Instead of running down into the river, Bhama had cut across the elephant's path and run straight up the steep incline. By the time the elephant had finished with the leader the youngster had traversed the gorge from above the beast and run along the path till he had come to the fork where they had rested. He stopped to catch his breath and then not hearing anyone, he decided that he would go up and wait at the spot where he had been christened into adulthood by his father before the start of the adventure.

By now the half moon had cast its dull halo on the track and Bhama had managed to climb the steep slope of the gorge with ease. Things had happened so fast that there had been no time to be frightened. But now as he waited for his people and knowing that at least one of them was dead, he started to shiver.

Then, sitting there alone, huddled against the rock, he knew the reason for his mother's suffering and her tears as he had left the house. He started to cry.

He waited for the sun to crest the hills before he took off again down into the gorge. The sight that met his eyes was his first encounter with tragedy. There was no sign of the elephant. His father was standing next to his uncle's dead body and the small group was in the process of performing the last rites before burying him.

He went straight to his father and hugged him. There were no tears for death was an integral part of their business. His uncle had not been the first to die and would not be the last either. More would succumb to the bush.

That day Bhama learnt the gravest lesson of his life. His father solemnly explained to him that when you are the acting leader and when the group is under threat, it is your duty to hold your position till you have assessed the threat and then take the action that you feel is best for the rest of the group.

His uncle could easily have run but if he had done that he would have compromised the position of the team behind him. Bhama would surely have died. Thus as he crouched low to figure out the exact course of action, he took the brunt of the attack. The elephant was too close and the charge had not given him time to think. He reacted selflessly and sacrificed himself to save the others.

They buried the noble man with full dignity. Each one in the group had touched the dead man's feet to absorb the immense courage that he had shown before gently lowering him into the grave. They buried him that morning and then hid the wood that they had been carrying.

Then they returned to the spot where they had stored the other logs, which was back up the face of the gorge in Madhumalai. That day they did another two rounds and moved another ten logs down into the gorge.

His father had cooked balls of ragi and squeezed the juice of the plentiful tamarind that grew wild in the gorge to make a curry. Bhama had been so distressed that he had not been able to eat anything. His father then explained to him that an honourable death is better than a dishonourable life. He said that it was better to die with honour than to be branded a cheat and a coward. The greatest crime in the forest was to break another person's trust. It showed weakness of character and this was an unjustifiable offence for the people of the jungle.

Bhama's uncle had died an honourable death, one about which the people of the jungle would reminisce for years to come. It was an act that would be written into the annals of tribal folklore.

***

They spent the whole of that day moving the wooden logs into position. His father gave the order to march just as the sun set. With Bhama trailing a close second, his father led the group up the face of the gorge.

They planned to cross the inhabited Mangala valley and then without being caught by the forest guards who live in the surrounding villages, to descend down the Barrenkatte track. This path would lead them to a motorable road where at exactly four in the morning a van would arrive to load the material. They would get their money on delivery.

His father explained that the buyer was an old and trusted businessman. He was a well-to-do person who had a dependable contact in Mangala and had good influence with the owners of sawmills in Gundulpet and Chamrajnagar. He said that this middleman could have the stolen wood regularized within a day of it landing in one of the mills.

But tonight they would have to do an extra load. He had promised the buyer seven pieces of teakwood. As they were short by one, instead of only one of them going back for a pickup he had decided to take the entire group down and bring back another full load of six logs from the cache that they had hidden in the gorge.

The rest of the journey back was uneventful and they soon returned for the second pickup. They descended back into the inky black gorge. It was only on their way back, whilst returning with the second load that they saw the light of the moon flood the valley. Bhama's father ascended the lip of the gorge and ordered a ten-minute halt. There they prayed together for the departed soul of his brother. For the first time in his life he was privy to the cry of seasoned poachers for it was only during prayer that the elders allowed themselves the liberty of tears. He was told then that displaying of emotion during prayer was acceptable, but only during prayer. Bhama allowed himself to cry all the way back.

Bhama was trailing his father by eight feet. This was the fastest and safest distance that they had arrived at through years of experience whilst carrying a log that is six feet in length and eighteen inches in diameter.

The duty of the team following is to look only at the person in front of him. It is the leader's job to look out for danger. Keeping a fix on his speed and maintaining the required distance was quite difficult on a jungle track at night. And so before Bhama knew it his log had crashed into his father's with force enough to drive the youngster off his feet.

His father who was leading had for some reason stopped dead in his tracks. Thus he had been expecting the youngster to come into him and had braced himself for the impact. He knew he could not afford to fall for standing just fifteen feet away, bathed in the blue light of the moon stood a huge tiger.

The leader knew that they had to stare down the big cat for if they showed the slightest hint of fear or flight, the cat would attack. They had blundered on the tiger's kill and he was in no mood to withdraw.

His father rumbled the soothing warning used by the hunters on sighting a tiger. Hearing this, the rest of the group had drawn to a halt. Only Bhama, not knowing what it meant, had blundered on.

Then his father spoke out in a loud and authoritative tone and ordered them to back off slowly. They did exactly that. Carefully they back-pedalled till they were out of the tiger's vision and then took off at a tangent, avoiding the big cat. All this was done without the least bit of fuss as if nothing had happened.

The tiger did not even growl and to Bhama, it seemed that the whole scene had been played out before, for both man and animal were quite comfortable with each other.

They arrived with their second load half an hour before their scheduled meeting. They dumped their smuggled goods in a drain next to the road and Bhama was asked to count and verify the number. It was twelve. His father explained that they would sell each piece for three hundred rupees and the loot would be shared according to seniority.

At exactly four that morning the buyer arrived. As he got out of the vehicle, Bhama recognized the small and wiry man straightaway for he had seen him around in the valley. He greeted him with a respectful bow. He knew that the man was highly influential in the powerful circles that mattered. The man looked at him approvingly and congratulated his father on producing a fine youngster for their thriving business.

He took out a bundle of notes and threw it in Bhama's direction. The young tribal caught the bundle of money and for the first time felt the comfort of holding thick sheafs of beautiful crisp paper in his hands. He caressed the notes before handing the bundle over to his father.

His father did not bother to count the notes, he knew that the bundle contained more money than their rightful due. The buyer looked at Bhama's father and said that the balance was for his brother who had died. There were no spoken condolences or apologies, just the simple acceptance of the passing away of a good soul. All matters of money were handled with great dignity. Nothing brings more solace to a widow than the sight of the thick bundles.

Bhama was shocked that the man knew that his uncle had been killed when no one had uttered a word about it. After the buyer left he asked his father how he had known this. His father merely said, 'Son those are the ways of the jungle.' Maybe the Tamilian clan of smugglers found the grave and read the signs or maybe the man put the facts together and concluded that one of them was dead for his brother was the leader and till that day had never missed an appointment. It is uncommon for a group to deliver extra at such meetings for the tribal runs the risk of bringing the wood out of the forest without knowing that the buyer has the means of disposing of it. This increases the risk for both. The only time that such rules are broken is when something sad or dastardly happens and the group needs more money. At such moments the buyer knows that by accepting more than he had ordered, he is only cementing their bond. With this in mind he invests in his future by giving extra for the bereaved family.

His father counted out the notes and handed each tribal his due. Bhama got his share of the loot and for the first time in his life pocketed three brand new hundred rupee notes.

The buyer had given a bundle of ten thousand. After removing the share of the rest of the group, Bhama's father was left with the princely sum of six thousand four hundred rupees for his sister-in-law.

Thus Bhama's bloody induction into adulthood was complete. Bhama first went to his aunt's house and gave her his own share of the money, then he returned home. That night for the last time in his life he went to his mother and slept in her arms. And that night his mother wept the night through for she knew she had lost her son to the jungles.

***

Bhama grew up in the drastically changing systems of the new world. When he was only five years old his tribe had been asked to leave the forests. Each family was given a meagre two acres of barren land with no water to cultivate and no means of ploughing it. The money that the tribals made from working with the forest department took care only of their daily livelihood. For them to expand on their land holdings or to buy a few oxen to till their land, they needed to raise some money. Thus his father had used his knowledge of the forest and started an illegal business of trading in precious timber with his elder brother as a partner.

Over a period of two years, they had built a dedicated and trusted team. Together they travelled vast distances, disappearing for weeks on end.

Bhama's mother used to get terribly agitated in the initial stages of their illegal activity but time soothed her nerves and after a few years, she would only pray once at night for their safe return before going to sleep.

That was till her brother-in-law had died. His was the first death that had occurred and it had shattered her newfound confidence in her husband's business. She had begged her husband to disband his team and live a life like the others. She even pointed out to him that now they had their own fields, well over fifty acres, their own house and even their own cows and oxen.

When they had dug the borewell on their land, she had stopped going for work to the forest department as they had started to question her on how they had got the money to dig the well. It was clear that the department had begun to suspect that her husband was the smuggler responsible for the extermination of teak and rosewood trees east of the state highway in the Bandipur Park. She would keep quiet and come home a disheartened woman for she knew that something bad was bound to happen sooner or later, if he continued with his smuggling activities. Then when she had stopped going to work, the range officer had come to their house and inquired why she was not working any more. She had lied that she was pregnant but she had known that the officer knew the truth – he knew that their family did not need the money from the department any more.

When her son also left the house for the jungles and her brother-in-law died and she saw the distraught widow's face, she decided that enough was enough. She threatened her husband that if the group did not stop its activity immediately, she would go straight to the police and spill the beans.

The death of his brother had had a profound effect on Bhama's father. He declared to the group that he would never again enter the forest for any illegal activity and that he was planning to join the forest department's intelligence cell. He would go to them and explain the method of operation of the poachers and smugglers of the area. He requested his group to do the same and join him. To his surprise, they accepted. That each of them was by now the owner of a house, cultivable fields and livestock must have helped them in taking this decision. They wanted to retire on the right side of the law.

But it was too late for the younger generation.

So saying the man finished his third reefer and asked for a cup of tea. By this time I was well into the story and wanted to know how this tale had ended. Taking small sips of his tea the man continued his narration.

Bhama had already got a taste of the pleasures of ill-gotten gains and had started to form a group of bold and able youngsters to join him, even as his father went across to the department as an informer. The forest department welcomed the father with open arms for they knew that this man's experience in the line of smuggling would help them in controlling the rampant poaching and smuggling that had started in various areas of the park.

Thus it came about that Bhama became the leader of a small band of eight youngsters. Initially they followed the known routes but when they realized that his father had effectively managed to control the tracks that they had used before, Bhama took it upon himself to find newer and more accessible routes. He decided to increase his supply base to other areas of the forest and thus established new routes and new buyers.

He led his people through numerous elephant charges. Some he withstood and some he ordered his band to run from. But every time that an elephant attacked, Bhama made sure that he was the last person out of the danger area.

Soon he became one of the most trusted people to lead in the forest. His ability to understand the animal's mind earned him great respect and even people from the surrounding jungles came to him to join his core group. He was always suspicious of new entrants for he never knew which one was a plant by his father.

One day he received an order for a hundred and twenty teakwood pieces. He knew that the size of the order required that they be supplied from Madhumalai. Such numbers were not easily available for smugglers in Bandipur. Thus he would have to use the same route through the Moyar where his uncle had died.

Having established different exit routes and the required pickup vehicles, he arranged for six groups of ten persons to do two trips each into the jungle.

He would lead his group of ten into the Moyar gorge via the Kathenburra stream. Other groups would be working in different zones within the same area and would have separate exit routes.

He descended with his team into the gorge once again but this time he was the leader. They proceeded to the logging point and having cut down their share of twenty solid teakwood logs, he collected the first lot of ten and took off for the return.

They had waded across the stream and were going along the Moyar heading for the track back up the northern face of the gorge when they heard the loud crack of a rifle. The group threw their load of teakwood and dived for cover. Then Bhama realized that the shot had not been fired at them but at something that was ahead of them.

Then he heard the thundering sound of a thousand hoofs approaching them from the east. He knew that a gaur stampede had started and that an entire herd of these large and powerful animals was running up-river. His team was in the direct path of the stampede.

The walls of the gorge were too steep to climb at this spot but the river was quite wide. Knowing that they did not have enough time to run, he ordered all the logs of wood to be assembled in front of them as one large pile.

Even as the last log was jammed into place and the ten men clambered behind the makeshift barrier, the charging gaur turned the final bend and headed straight for them. Bhama knew then that the stampede was a planned move by the person who had fired the shot. The men clung to each other in order to avoid getting pulled into the fast approaching melee. A female was leading the herd and when she was but a few yards from the pile of wood she darted into the gap to her right. The animal to her left knew that it could not squeeze past the wooden logs and decided to cut sharp left. The movement of these two leading females decided the fate of the ten men huddled behind the logs. The entire herd parted as it passed the logs barely a few feet away from the cowering men.

Bhama was so elated at the success of his idea that he hollered in delight and slapped the animals as they darted past. Then asking his team to get back on the Tamil Nadu side of the stream he crept forward through the broken bush to look for the person responsible for starting the deadly stampede. He saw a figure right on top of the gorge. Even from that distance he recognized the walk. It was his father.

That night he did not climb the gorge in the usual place but retraced back a few kilometres till he came to the Rolling Rock Falls. There he led the ascent up the gorge and headed straight for Bandipur. They walked past Betadekatte, past the Mangala dam straight into Bisonpura and then instead of turning east towards Burrenkatte he headed straight for Menakemanahalli. Just before the final hill he cut north and approached the road that led to the KSTDC hotel. He stopped a kilometre short of the hotel and ordered his men to hide the logs that they had carried with them, under the culvert. Then he walked to the hotel and made a call to Gundulpet changing the pickup point for that night.

After seeing his father in the gorge he was positive that the normal routes would be heavily guarded. Thus he had decided to head through an area where his father would least expect him and what better place than under his very nose?

They doubled back on the same route and brought the remaining ten pieces of teak logs to complete their quota. Bhama delivered the full 120 pieces and went home with a substantial profit that night.

His greatness was in his ability to distribute his wealth. He would share his profits with all the people of the Mangala valley. He preferred to work in Mangala because most of his movement of materials was through this valley. Also because he had made a house in the hamlet.

When teak and rosewood became scarce he started on sandalwood. He had picked up a substantial order of sandal core, which had to be delivered to a pre-fixed destination in Kerala.

This time his team consisted of one large group of thirteen runners. They cut the trees in Anaikatti on the eastern edge of Madhumalai and having crossed the Moyar he decided to take the cross cut directly into Kerala. They came up near the circular road and then crossed over into sand road. Here they proceeded for an hour along the Kakkanhalla stream and it was only the special precaution that he took when transporting sandal, of keeping a scout in front of the carriers, that saved their precious timber load and kept them from a definite jail sentence.

It was a full moon night and the scout who had been running higher than the portage group, on the upper ridge of an adjacent hill, had caught a glimpse of reflecting moonlight on metal. He knew straightaway that they were heading into a trap. He had bellowed back the gravest signal of them all, the mating call of the tiger. He did it thrice and then waited for a few seconds. Then he repeated it again.

The moment Bhama heard the 'Oooonhhh! Ooonh! Oonh' call float across the hill he stopped and bade his mates to hide in the thick forest bordering the stream. Their orders were clear – if the task force attacked from the Tamil Nadu side they were to cross over into Karnataka and make good their escape and if the Karnataka Special Task Force were to attack, then they should drop their load and run deep into the opposite jungle.

He answered his friend in the low answering moan of a tigress. Then he made his way to his friend, keeping to the thicket at all times. His entire team was wearing deep olive green clothes. He insisted that the shirts be full sleeves. He knew from experience that the free-swinging movement of the dark brown skin of their arms was a sure giveaway, for an experienced eye could pick it out from a long distance.

He met up with the scout and crept closer to the unsuspecting police force. When he got to within fifty yards he assessed the situation. And straightaway knew that it was the superbly trained Tamil Nadu Special Task Force that was hidden along the track. He also knew that this trap could only have been set on a tip off by an insider for he had not used the commonly used track that most runners do. He felt the hair on his neck stand as realization hit him that no one outside the group had known of their whereabouts and only if someone were following them could they have informed the police of the route that he had decided to take.

He was not called the chameleon for nothing. He picked up his load and cutting north headed for the heart of Bandipur. This time instead of keeping the scout he decided to give his load to him and fell back to lay a few traps of his own.

He fixed a place where the group should rest and where they should wait for him irrespective of how late he was. Then in complete silence he fell to work. He set up four snares along the path that he had taken. Two were hanging noose traps tied to a thick whippy branch and two were the standard jaw clamp traps used to catch larger prey. Next to the last metal snare he left his insignia with a note stating that if any of the others dared to come further a 'stick in the groin' awaited them. This was nothing but a pointed and sharp spring-loaded stump, triggered by a rope that lay across the path. It was designed to drive deep into the lower belly.

He completed his work in half an hour and then after adding the last finishing touches and satisfied with what he had done, he took off in a fast lope after his team. He had hardly gone half a kilometre when he heard the shrieking cries of one of his pursuers. The clamp trap had shut hard on the legs of one of them. Minutes later he heard the mangled cry of distress as another member of the posse was whipped back and left screaming high up in the trees.

He knew then that the rest of the trip would be uneventful. And it was. He also knew that it could only have been the people of the dreaded smuggler with the twirling big moustache who could have dared tread on his path. The smugglers from Gopinath thought that sandalwood and ivory was their sole right and prerogative and nobody else had any claim to this trade. He knew that one day he would have to sign a peace treaty with these people but till then he would keep the substantial largesse for himself.

Keeping Gopalswamy Betta to their north, they headed west. Bhama kept to the north of the Chamanaholla road. Luckily due to the rains the undergrowth was thick and they could travel well into the morning without the fear of being caught. It was a two-night trek and he planned to spend the first night in the bush barely a kilometre and a half from the Kalkerre camp.

Not wanting to travel in daylight, they stopped at six in the morning and rested. Bhama took over the lookout's post till the afternoon as his team slept. He changed guard at four and soon returned to his temporary camp and fell asleep. He woke to the feeling of a heavy weight moving across his legs. In the late evening light he saw a very large and heavy snake gliding over him. With terror gripping his heart he noticed that it was a king cobra. He knew that one bite from its huge sacks of poison would mean instant death. He also knew that whereas a regular cobra might not be able to deliver a lethal dose through his thick blanket, the fangs of this reptile were so long that they would pierce through the quilt that he had on with supreme ease. He froze and allowed the huge serpent to pass. His men could do nothing as the reptile rippled over their boss. In the jungle the passing of a snake over a man is considered a good omen and the men relaxed after it had slipped away in search of other snakes to eat.

Late that night, using the light of the moon, Bhama shot a langur and they ate the brain of the monkey. Early next morning at the break of the false dawn, on the scheduled hour they reached their destination.

Bhama collected a hefty sum from a well-oiled Malayali of small stature. The Malayali took him aside and said that he had heard of a trap that was laid for him but he had had no way of informing him. One of the Gopinath clan had called a buyer who had reported the matter to the Tamil Nadu Task Force. He had a source within the buyer's office and was told of the trap. Bhama knew then they would have to move their logging of sandalwood into the core zone of Bandipur, which in any case was closer to the Kerala border. But he was furious at the Gopinath clan for setting him up. They could have confronted him in Madhumalai and come to a settlement. His father had not wanted to take on the Gopinath clan and thus had resisted handling sandalwood. But he was different. The trip to Kerala was so successful that soon he had a regular supply of sandalwood running across the border.

Within six months, Bhama had established a flourishing illegal trade in smuggling sandalwood to Kerala and teak and rosewood to different parts of Mysore and Chamrajnagar districts.

One matter that really roused his ire was how his people were being used by the middlemen who would buy the wood for a pittance and then sell it for huge profits in the major metropolitan markets like Bangalore and Mysore. He realized that he and his followers were allowing the mill owners to get fat from the juices of their hard work whilst they risked death for a few thousand rupees. Apart from capture by the police or the forest department, they had to risk the denizens of the jungle.

Thus as his supply of wood from the forests increased so did his price. Because he was supplying such high quality wood, the people dealing with him did not complain. He explained to his tribal suppliers that no one in the whole area of eastern Bandipur should supply a single piece of wood without his knowledge. And if anybody wanted money they should come to him. This they did and he made sure that he dealt with them all fairly. Thus over a period of one year, he abolished the middleman and secured all the profits for his people.

It was only a matter of time before his ill-gotten wealth started to get the acceptance that it so easily does in a Third World country. If a person makes enough money by beating the system, then malevolent sentiment soon turns into benevolent respect.

He became a master of tricks. He never delivered at one given spot and always had three lorries going out for collection at any given time. Only one would be loaded and the other two would be dummy runs. Even the truck drivers did not know till the end as to who would get the load.

He set up hideouts in the caves of the forest and cached food, clothing, blankets and bedding in each of these dens. He established a complex set of warning calls that his team would use indicating the type and seriousness of threat.

And most important of all, he stopped the movement of the Gopinath clan from poaching or smuggling within his area. He kept lookouts at strategic places and the moment they saw the slightest disturbance they would report the matter to him. He would take stern and immediate action.

He trained his people in trapping animals and soon they became experts at handling the different traps. There was hardly ever a day when his people went without meat.

He never quite forgot the death of his uncle and his loathing of the elephant grew with his power. One day after a long discussion with his mates he decided that he would acquire a gun. Jaga, his most trusted friend said that they should not get into poaching as that would lead them into a huge network of deceit and cheating. Selling ivory and skins of animals was tough business and considered a bad omen by their tribe. Bhama agreed with his friend but still felt that he, being the leader of the tribe, should acquire a gun.

Here the young storyteller paused as a group of five elephants had just walked into the water and after drinking had started to wallow in the slush. We waited for the pachyderms to complete their pleasurable routine and as they departed to feed on the periphery of the waterhole, and after a fresh round of tea and onion pakodas had been served, he continued in a low whisper.

It was during his forays into the towns and villages that he met a child of the city who had come wandering into the jungles. The first time they met the city dweller requested Bhama to take him out for a walk and show him some elephants. The boy from the city had been so impressed by

Bhama's knowledge of animal movements that he had asked him to join his company and said that he would pay him a healthy amount of money every month. The tribal had no idea why this young city dwelling person would want to pay money to see wild animals. He was suspicious at first but the pay was good and he decided to join the youngster, if only to see what it was all about.

The youngster soon opened a small tourist resort and Bhama realized that it was not only this young man, even foreigners would crave to see the animals of the forest. The tips were great and the food, clothing and medical expenses were free for him and his family. The benefits of staying on in the youngster's company grew with time. Bhama stayed on.

I felt my nerves tingle as I surmised that the youngster from the city that he was speaking of could only be me, but who was this Bhama?

The man continued his story as though oblivious of the question that was buzzing in my mind.

People from nearby villages would often question Bhama on whether he had seen the dreaded smuggler of the Mangala valley and at the same time visitors to the resort would inquire if he had met up with the dreaded bandit Veerappan and whether he could show them a few samples of the teak and rosewood that this person was after. Bhama never answered the questions and always acted as though he knew nothing. He would try and search for a tree to please the foreigners, who if satisfied would pay huge tips before they left.

Bhama soon came to accept that there was money in preserving and conserving the jungles and its animals.

One day, taking leave from his boss, he went to his father and fell at his feet. He said that he had been wrong in carrying on the illegal activity even after his father's group had been disbanded. He apologized for going against the system that his father had tried to establish and asked for forgiveness.

That was the first day that the people of Mangala saw his father cry. His mother looked at him with love and cried along with her husband as he strode out of the house. For the first time in her life her tears were those of joy.

Bhama disbanded his group of trusted followers and absorbed them in his fight for the survival of the species that till recently he had been responsible for killing.

As our narrator came to the end of his story, I saw tears in his eyes and he turned to me and said, 'Sir, like Bhama I have had enough of this smuggling business. Please help me settle down and start on a new life.' Saying this he fell at my feet and wouldn't let go till I had promised him that I would do my best to see that he get on the path of earning a legitimate source of income. I asked him to meet me at Bush Betta.

Today I would like to believe that this person will come back to me. Only time will tell whether he will or not but what I do know for sure is that I am unlikely to see him again until he has earned enough from the forest to see him live as comfortable a life as the fabled Bhama of his story.

***

Till today, I do not know the true identity of Bhama. Could it have been Nanju? I do not believe it was, for I know Nanju too well and I am sure that somewhere in our relationship he would have slipped up and I would have learnt the truth. Besides, when he came to work for me, Nanju had hardly any wealth. Even today, all he possesses is a small house and a couple of acres of land that hardly equal the kind of riches that the hero of the story was supposed to have.

I do believe that persons like Bhama exist, and it is possible that maybe one of them did come to Bush Betta and earn an honest living for a while. I say for a while because there is no one in the camp at present that fits the bill. If 'Bhama' was with us for a few weeks or months before moving on, I can only hope that the time he spent with us was enough to change his mindset, and show him that there are other ways of making money than destroying the trees and animals of the forest.

Epilogue

By all ye cry or whisper, by all ye leave or do,
The silent sullen peoples, shall weigh your gods and you ...

– Rudyard Kipling

I have had a wonderful time living in the forest, amongst its wilderness and its people. Yes, life has been tough and we have had to fight our way through most of it but the satisfaction that I have gained from watching the tribals of the valley, looking at the world with newfound pride, their eyes reflecting the knowledge that they are now free for they are able to fend for themselves and their families, is fulfilment enough. Watching the deer feed in peace from our doorstep, hosting the elusive leopard in one of our rooms, hearing the tiger roar its freedom and pleasure from across the hills, having the elephants use our pool for a quick bath has given me more pleasure than anything else in the world. It has confirmed our success in protecting them from man. Though our journey in the wilds has just begun, today I feel that I have travelled many a mile and achieved something of what I set out to do .

The jungle has taught me one important lesson in life.

That life, death, remorse, happiness, sadness, elation, nervousness and jubilation are all one and the same. The uncomplicated wilderness free from the politics and pressures of the world, where existence is in plain black or white, where you either live or die has truly simplified the meaning of life for me. At times I fear that it may have oversimplified matters to such an extent that city dwellers find me odd!

When I view the past twenty years of my life, I can say with complete honesty that ever since I gave up cricket, the forests have been the only obsession that has given me the impetus to perform with as much fervour as I would have done, had I still been playing the game. Because good work in sensitive areas like ecology that is essential in Third World countries, is appreciated and respected, the media coverage makes people believe that those of us working in these sectors are loaded financially – unfortunately it is far from the case. We are rich in zeal and emotions and money to us wildlifers is but a necessity, not a passion.

Today, Sangeeta and I live in Bangalore with our children. Regular bridge and golf whenever I am in the city keeps me in touch with the normal world. Work in the bush continues and with each setting sun – for the rising sun I never seem to see – I thank god for giving me all that I ever dreamt of.

I would like to end with a few thoughts on conservation. Is eco-tourism the necessary utilization of tourism as the integral tool for conservation and protection of the environment? Believe me in a Third World country where the existing laws are easily compromised by the lure of money; when Transparency International's 2004 Global Corruption Barometer lists India on number five, eco-tourism in its truest form with its alternate revenues that take nothing from the forest, can regularly overcome forces that normal management cannot even address without taking anything away from the forest.

One objective of this book is to help generate the much required awareness so essential to establish eco-tourism as the integral tool for conservation in India. And I hope that those amongst you planning an eco-tourism development will do it for the right reasons and beliefs. If you want to go into the fragile environment only to better the financial bottom lines for yourselves or your shareholders then please think again. Nothing is worth the loss of our incredible environmental heritage. In this beautiful, raw and at most times savage yet sensitive and gentle wilderness, it is the duty of each and every one of us to give rather than take – for our environment is under severe pressure from man and man alone. The challenge lies in protecting the world that we live in from ourselves – our own greed. Eco-tourism is a way of life. It is a philosophy that needs to be lived. It cannot be a stand-alone business and people should not try and make it one.

All this is easier said than done. I have worked in the forests for over eighteen years. I have also been on the wildlife advisory board of the state and have in my work had the privilege of meeting numerous celebrities in the field of conservation. I have asked them all one simple question, just one question to which till very recently I did not get an answer.

My question to them was, 'How does one tell a tribal, who has had his mother killed and his house plundered by an elephant, his small field of a few acres stripped of its cultivation by the animals from the forests, his cattle repeatedly devoured by the tiger, that let alone not kill these brutes he should go out of his way and help in their protection?'

The answer was not given by the cerebral lot for they had none that would convince a poor villager; but it came in the form of a nondescript man from the jungles, my friend Nanju. After having worked with him for a few years, I managed to convert him into a life that solely depended on the forests but took nothing from it. Where earlier he would cut and sell wood, collect honey or other forest produce, and a few of his tribe would trap animals and sell their skin and meat, today he protects the same with total dedication. All because he gets paid for showing the tourists the very same animal that his people would have killed a few years ago.

This understanding, this awareness and return to the local person, in my view is what will finally save our forests and our wildlife. It is when the local populace decides that protection is better than plundering, that we will arrive on the right path to saving our entire ecosystem and saving this truly incredible and wonderful world of ours from ourselves.

I quote a famous poet:

Bante rahe bigarte rahe karobare shouq
Ek hum jo arzoo ka sahare bane rahe

My aspirations of desire, they make and they wreck
As I live on with hope as my support.

These lines pretty much denote both Sangeeta's and my life in the bush and our fight for survival in the jungles. Both of us have so many aspirations but so little time to fulfil them but we continue to strive with hope as our support.